FURIOUS

DANIEL KOLENDA

CHARISMA HOUSE

Furious by Daniel Kolenda
Published by Charisma House, an imprint of Charisma Media
1150 Greenwood Blvd., Lake Mary, Florida 32746

For more resources like this, visit MyCharismaShop.com and the author's website at cfan.org.

Cataloging-in-Publication Data is on file with the Library of Congress.
International Standard Book Number: 978-1-63641-514-7
E-book ISBN: 978-1-63641-515-4

1 2025
Printed in the United States of America

DEDICATION

TO MY BELOVED wife, the joy of my life, Elizabeth Kolenda—

You have been my unwavering support, my greatest encourager, and my most faithful intercessor. While I've pored over pages, engrossed, you've kept me grounded. While I've written late into the night and early in the morning, hunched over the little desk in our room, you've never once complained. Instead, you've prayed, listened, and brought me an endless stream of coffee (my addiction, one of your many ministries). You've been my sounding board—endlessly patient as I read and reworked these words, always willing to hear them again.

You are the epitome of a godly woman—walking in the Spirit, bearing fruit in ways so practical and real that they leave no doubt about the source. You embody grace, not just in word, but in quiet, faithful action. Love, joy, peace, patience, kindness, goodness, faithfulness, gentleness, and self-control—they're not abstract virtues in you. They live; they breathe; they serve.

This book is a battle cry for freedom, for life in the Spirit, and for grace that cannot be earned. I have seen all these things, first and best, in you.

Thank you for choosing me.

CONTENTS

PREFACE

A LETTER BEFORE THE LETTER

One of my lifelong dreams has been to preach through the entire Bible, expositorily, before I die. Seems unlikely at my current pace. I tend to linger too long—like a bee setting out to fly over a field of wildflowers but getting captivated by each. If only there were more time.

It doesn't help when I don't just stop to savor a flower; I set up camp and write a book about it. And that's exactly what happened here.

After all, I figure, I've done the pressing, the straining, the hard work of drawing it out. I might as well share the nectar I've been savoring.

Anyway, here's the story. I was preaching through Galatians, walking my church—Nations Church in Orlando, Florida—through it verse by verse. Every week, people would come up to me wide-eyed, shaking their heads, telling me how much it was changing them.

I wasn't surprised.

Galatians is that kind of letter. It isn't neat. It isn't polished. It isn't safe.

It's urgent, fiery, raw. The kind of letter you write when everything is on the line—when people you love are being led astray and you don't have time for pleasantries.

New Testament scholar Craig Keener calls it a letter that

"seethes with negative emotion."[1] And it does. Paul isn't just teaching—he's pleading, rebuking, fighting. Every word drips with urgency.

This isn't doctrine from a distance. These are battle cries. A man standing in the gap, refusing to let the gospel be distorted, refusing to let people be bound in chains that Christ already shattered.

Galatians has been called the Christian Magna Carta, the Declaration of Independence of the faith. It isn't measured. It isn't calm. It burns with fire, emotion, and yes, even anger. Paul is livid because the very heart of the gospel is under attack.

This was the book that set fire to Martin Luther's bones, igniting the Protestant Reformation. Luther famously called Galatians "my epistle," saying it was as dear to him as his own wife, Catherine von Bora[2]—high praise, considering she brewed his beer and debated theology with him at the dinner table.

And even now, wherever revival is breaking out across the world, you will find the echoes of Paul's words: "*Did you receive the Spirit by works of the law or by hearing with faith?*" (Gal. 3:2).

So when my sermon series on Galatians ended, I set out to write a simple commentary. Something useful, something my congregation could reflect on. But the more I wrote, the more something felt off. It was too clean. Too clinical. And Galatians is neither.

I kept picturing Paul—not as a scholar behind a desk, but as a man pacing the floor, eyes flashing, hands gripping the edge of the table as he dictated this letter to his scribe.

And then it hit me.

This wasn't just a letter. It was a moment. A moment in history when everything hung in the balance.

I didn't just want to explain Galatians. I wanted you to *feel* it.

So I imagined it. What if we could sit in the same room with Paul as he dictated this letter? What if we could hear his voice, see his scars, sense the fire in his soul?

That's how *Furious* was born.

So what is this? A novel? A commentary? A devotional?

Well, truth is, it's all of the above. But with a unique twist.

This isn't dry exposition. Yes, there are some lengthy endnotes (and honestly, some of them are pretty fascinating), but I've kept them out of the main text so you stay immersed in the story.

You'll step into a room—a dimly lit space where parchment and ink sit ready, where a man with scars on his body paces the floor, dictating words that will change history. You'll experience Galatians the way it was first received: as a letter, urgent and alive, dictated by a man on fire with conviction.

Galatians isn't just history. It isn't just theology. It's the beating heart of the gospel.

And now, I invite you to step inside it.

Pull up a chair. Watch as the ink dries under the flickering lamplight.

Listen as Paul's message unfolds with clarity—*his* words, *his* fire, *his* fight. And I pray that as you do, this letter—this furious, unrelenting defense of grace—will do its work in you too.

This is *Furious: A Modern Retelling of Paul's Fight for the Gospel.*

Enjoy!

—Daniel Kolenda

INTRODUCTION

THE NEWS CAME late. Two years late.

Slavery in the United States had been legally abolished with the Emancipation Proclamation, signed by President Abraham Lincoln on January 1, 1863. From that moment on, every enslaved person was, by law, free. The war had been fought. The victory had been declared. But not everyone wanted to let go.

In Texas, far from the front lines, 250,000 men, women, and children still lived in bondage because their captors refused to release them. Their masters kept them in ignorance, robbing them of their rightful freedom, holding them in chains that no longer had any legal claim over them.

So the government sent armed messengers to deliver the news.

On June 19, 1865, General Gordon Granger stood on the balcony of Ashton Villa and read aloud General Order No. 3: "*The people of Texas are informed that, in accordance with a proclamation from the Executive of the United States, all slaves are free....*"

It was a declaration. A proclamation. A moment that changed history.

Some people collapsed where they stood, overcome by the weight of it. Some wept, holding loved ones close. Others stared in stunned silence, as if waiting for someone to tell them it wasn't true. It had been true for a long time. But now, at last, they could live it.

Paul's letter to the Galatians is a Juneteenth moment for the church.

The gospel had set them free—declared them righteous, not by law, not by works, but by faith in Christ alone. Yet legalists crept in, whispering, *"You're not really free. Not unless you keep the law. Not unless you do more. Not unless you measure up."*

And Paul wouldn't have it. This letter isn't a gentle reminder. It's a rescue mission. A battle cry. It's not neat and tidy. It's urgent, fiery, raw. Paul doesn't ease in with pleasantries. He doesn't build his case slowly. He kicks down the door.

"I am shocked that you are turning away so soon from God, who called you to himself through the loving mercy of Christ" (Gal. 1:6).

It's the voice of a man fighting for something precious. Fighting for people who had tasted freedom but were being dragged back into slavery.

Legalism didn't die in the first century. It's alive and well, creeping into the church today just as it did in Galatia.

There's a growing trend—maybe you've seen it—of believers feeling like faith in Christ isn't quite enough. Some go so far as to take on the yoke of the Mosaic Law, convinced that righteousness is found in Sabbath-keeping, dietary restrictions, or observing Jewish festivals. Some even dress like Orthodox Jews, wearing tzitzit, covering their heads with kippahs, calling Jesus by a Hebrew name, as if returning to the old covenant brings them closer to God.

Paul would have flipped tables over this.

Not because the Law was bad—it wasn't. It was holy, righteous, and good. But it was never meant to be a path to righteousness. It was a signpost, a shadow, a tutor to lead us to Christ. To go back to it as a means of justification is to say, in effect, *"Jesus, Your sacrifice wasn't enough. I'll take it from here."*

That's not just dangerous. It's damning.

But legalism isn't always so obvious. It's not just in fringe movements. It's not just in Hebrew Roots theology or fundamentalist sects. It's everywhere.

It's in every false religion, every man-made system that says righteousness must be earned. Hinduism, Islam,

Mormonism—they're all built on the same foundation: works-based righteousness.

And before we start pointing fingers at cults and religious systems, let's be honest—it creeps into our own hearts too.

You don't have to be wearing a yarmulke or keeping kosher to be a legalist.

Legalism is subtle. Insidious. Persistent.

It's the guilt-ridden believer who won't pray because they've had a "bad week."

It's the perfectionist who believes God loves them a little less when they fail.

It's the minister who measures their worth in attendance numbers and sermon views.

It's the Christian who feels anxious after missing morning devotions, as if their standing with God hinges on flawless discipline.

It's the weary believer, exhausted from trying to be "good enough."

Legalism doesn't just put chains on people's bodies—it binds their souls.

We struggle because we think *there must be something more we can do.* We fear that grace is *too* good, *too* free, *too* risky. What if it's misunderstood? What if people abuse it?

Paul saw this hesitation coming. In Romans 6, he confronts it head-on:

> What shall we say then? Shall we continue in sin that grace may abound?
>
> —ROMANS 6:1, NKJV

Dr. Martyn Lloyd-Jones put it this way:

> The true preaching of the gospel of salvation by grace alone always leads to the possibility of this charge being brought against it. There is no better test as to whether a

> man is really preaching the New Testament gospel than this, that some people might misunderstand it.[1]

In other words, if it doesn't seem scandalous, it might not be grace at all.

Yes, grace is radical—but it's not up for negotiation. It's God's idea, not ours. He's the One who designed it to be this audacious, this free, this offensive to human pride.

And that's precisely the problem. Deep down, we prefer what we can control. Human nature wants a system we can measure, something we can contribute to—so we can take at least a little credit. We instinctively reach for effort, discipline, and performance, not because they can save us but because they make us *feel* safe.

If we're honest, grace—wild, untamed grace—scares us.

But grace only feels frightening until you see it clearly. When the Spirit opens your eyes—when grace becomes more than a doctrine and turns into a revelation—it no longer threatens your sense of control; it liberates you from it. Grace isn't a license to sin; it's the path to the Spirit. And the Spirit doesn't just comfort us; He empowers us to live in freedom. In fact, He's the only way.

That's the revelation at the heart of Galatians. It confronts our fear of grace, our need to control, our tendency to drift back into law. It lifts our eyes to the sufficiency of Christ and the power of the Spirit. And that's why Galatians isn't just a book for the past. It's for right now.

For the weary believer who wonders if they've done enough.

For the rule-follower who secretly hopes their discipline earns them favor.

For the Christian who loves grace in theory but still lives like their salvation depends on them.

For the seeker, worn out by religion, longing for peace but never finding rest.

For the devoted follower of another faith, striving endlessly to please God.

Paul writes with fire in his bones, fighting for our freedom—not just from the Law of Moses but from every performance-driven, works-based, self-justifying lie that tries to drag us back into slavery.

Galatians is a battle cry for every generation—a declaration that Jesus alone is enough.

His grace is enough.

His finished work is enough.

The war is over. The chains are broken. The debt is paid.

So why do we still live like captives?

Why do so many believers—already free—still labor under the weight of chains that Christ shattered long ago?

It's Juneteenth all over again.

The gospel went out—the Emancipation Proclamation of heaven—declaring freedom to all who believe. Yet still some live in bondage.

Some are held back by ignorance, never having heard the truth.

Others are deceived by those who profit from their captivity.

And some, tragically, know they are free but still live like slaves, shackled by old fears, old systems, old ways of thinking.

And Paul? He's the soldier, marching into enemy-occupied territory, reading the decree aloud, shaking men and women awake, declaring with holy defiance: "You are free! Now live like it!"

Get ready…

The battle for the gospel is about to begin.

How to Read This Book

Paul's letter to the Galatians isn't a quiet, scholarly treatise. It's urgent, passionate—written in the heat of battle. And because of that, this book isn't a typical commentary.

Instead of dry exposition, *Furious* invites you into the room where history was made. You'll step into the setting, watch the ink dry, and hear the conversation unfold as Paul dictates his letter to a scribe.

That scribe, in this book, is Tertius.

In Romans 16:22, he makes a brief cameo, signing off with a personal greeting—evidence that he was the one transcribing Paul's words. Did he write Galatians too? We don't know. But we do know that Paul used scribes frequently (1 Cor. 16:21; Gal. 6:11; Col. 4:18), relying on them to preserve his letters.

Tertius, in this retelling, plays a crucial role—not just as Paul's recorder, but as his conversation partner. He asks the kinds of questions you and I might ask. He reacts with wonder, frustration, and conviction. He challenges, presses for clarity, and at times struggles to keep up. Through their exchange, we don't just read Paul's words—we enter them.

History remembers Paul's name, but behind every letter was a faithful scribe—an unseen hand preserving words that would outlive empires.

Tertius represents all of them: the scribes, the recorders, the quiet servants who shaped the written Word that would build the church for generations.

A Word About Creative License

While this book is rooted in Scripture, it is also a dramatization. In bringing Paul's letter to life, I've made certain narrative choices—imagining the setting, the dialogue, and even the emotional dynamics between Paul and Tertius.

At key moments—such as the timing of Paul's meeting with church leaders in Jerusalem, his journey to Arabia, his physical afflictions, or the way he confronted Peter—I've taken interpretive positions. These aren't random guesses but thoughtful reconstructions based on historical and textual possibilities. Still, they remain speculative.

My goal is not to settle these debates but to raise awareness of them—to help readers engage more deeply with the text. Even if the events didn't unfold exactly as I've described, I hope the narrative helps you feel the tension, urgency, and humanity behind the theology—and that it inspires further study, reflection, and conversation.

How the Book Is Structured

This book follows Galatians verse by verse, unfolding the text within the story itself.

- Each chapter begins with a title and the passage of Galatians it covers.
- Paul's actual words—the dictated portions of Galatians—are presented in bold font, with their references listed immediately after.
- At the end of each chapter, you'll find a QR code linking to a short devotional. These offer spiritual insight on part of the previous scene, with reflection, prayer, and a call to action—designed to help you personally engage with the themes of Galatians.

DANIELKOLENDA.COM/FURIOUS

- Everything else—the backstory, the explanations, the conversation between Paul and Tertius—serves to bring Paul's message to life, making sense of his words in real time.

By the time you finish *Furious*, you will have read through the entire Book of Galatians without even realizing it. You'll absorb its logic, emotion, and urgency in a way that feels natural—because that's how it was originally received.

A Note on Translation

For clarity and readability, this book primarily uses the New Living Translation (NLT), a version that captures the passion and force of Paul's words in plain, vibrant language. In places where the Greek wording adds depth, I reference it. And in rare cases, I diverge slightly from the NLT for clarity or emphasis—always with the goal of faithfulness to Paul's intent.

And now, as you step into this story, I invite you to listen—to hear Paul's voice as if for the first time.

The ink is fresh. The words are urgent. The battle for the gospel is real.

CHAPTER 1

THE FIGHT FOR THE GOSPEL

THE GULF OF Corinth stretched wide and clean, a pale wash of blue, cool and untouched by the heat of the coming day. One lonely seagull glided overhead, its white wings catching the first hints of gold as the sun sent its light skimming across the water.

Closer to shore, mist clung to the hills, and the dawn breeze carried the scent of damp earth and brine through an open window, stirring the silence inside a small, square room—where a short, stocky man sat motionless.

His thick beard and prominent eyebrows cast shadows over his face. His tunic, frayed and cinched at the waist with a leather belt, was layered under a faded cloak. His sandals, cracked and worn thin, had molded to the shape of his feet, bearing the dark imprints of heel and toe.

Paul was nearing fifty, but the lines on his weary face made him look much older. He leaned forward in a rough-hewn chair, lost in thought. His gaze fixed on the distant sea, eyes narrowing as if straining to see the horizon—though whether he truly could was uncertain. Yet beyond it, he saw with absolute clarity.

The space was unadorned—all purpose, no personality. The only entrance was a door fashioned from cedar planks, sanded smooth and bound with bronze fittings. Beneath the window, a plain wooden table stood bare. In its shadow lay a weathered leather sack, creased and tied shut: a traveler's companion, a keeper of things—perhaps of treasures, perhaps of secrets.

In the center of the room stood a heavy wooden writing table, square and worn with use. A second chair, this one empty, sat in front of it, back to the door, facing the window beyond. It was the writing chair—quiet, expectant, waiting.

To the right slumped a cold hearth with blackened stones, its past fires long extinguished. Nestled inside, a small bronze brazier glowed faintly, the embers inside pulsing with lazy heat. Above the hearth hung the room's sole decoration—a simple cross, its beams made from two rough branches, tied together where they intersected with a bit of fraying twine.

To the left, in the far corner, a triangular wooden shelf fit snugly into the angle of the walls, lined with lamps, wicks, and squat jars of oil—as if prepared for some nocturnal siege. A long bench, pressed against the wall by the threshold, held a wooden pitcher and two matching cups. Beside them, a vase overflowed with fresh-cut jasmine, poppies, and bougainvillea, their fragrance drifting through the room, mingling with the salty air.

This space wasn't much to look at, really, but to Paul it was perfect. He had always favored simplicity. Why clutter the mind with distractions? Especially now, when his thoughts needed room to breathe.

The small guesthouse where Paul sat was just one building within a sprawling compound. A manicured garden stretched between it and the main house, a stone path winding through the greenery to connect them.

The main house was grand but unpretentious, its spaciousness balanced by a quiet warmth. Its owner, Gaius, made no show of wealth—no extravagant art or gilded statues—though a few well-placed vases and tapestries lent a touch of refinement.

Every now and then Gaius threw open his doors and welcomed the entire church into his home. They called them love feasts—long, joy-filled gatherings on his estate beyond the city walls. His dwelling stood on a gentle rise in the valley, nestled between the hills that surrounded Corinth. From there, you could glimpse the gulf, where sunlight shimmered on the water like scattered gold. It was a long walk for many, but they came—drawn not just by the view, or the promise of a fine meal in a lavish home, but by the gracious host.

Gaius had a way of making people feel like family. His door was never closed, his table never empty. He welcomed the weary, embraced the lonely, and treated strangers like old friends. To know Gaius was to love him; to sit at his table, an honor. And now, his doors had opened once more, this time for Paul, who needed a place to work on a project of supreme importance.

Gaius had no idea what was about to happen under his roof. Even Paul probably didn't fully grasp it. He knew he would write to rescue a congregation from error. What he didn't know was that his words would do far more. They would steady the church for generations. They would echo across centuries. They would change the world.

Paul sat quietly, so absorbed in thought he nearly missed the soft footsteps approaching on the cobblestones outside. The door creaked open, and Gaius stepped inside, his broad frame filling the entryway. Morning light spilled in behind him, casting a long shadow across the floor. His graying beard framed a rugged face, but his welcoming smile softened the strength in his features.

A younger man stepped in beside him, clutching a leather-bound scroll as if it held all the secrets of the universe. His eyes darted around nervously, taking in the room, then flicking back to Gaius for reassurance.

"Good morning, Paul," Gaius said. "Here's Tertius, the one I was telling you about." Gaius gestured to the young man at his side. "He's the best scribe I know and a bit of a scholar too. He's recently come to faith in Jesus and is eager to serve."

Paul turned from the window, his sharp gaze locking onto Tertius. The young man stood poised, his expression composed and bright.

Of average height and a slim build, Tertius carried the air of a scholar—ink-stained fingers, a tunic marked with faint smudges, signs of long hours bent over parchment. He radiated energetic intelligence, as if his mind were always at work—analyzing, observing, seeking to understand.

Though Jewish by birth, his name—Tertius, meaning "third"—was distinctly Roman. Like many Jews in the empire, he carried both a Hebrew name and a Roman one, a personal name often assigned to freedmen, scribes, or those in administrative roles. His world had been shaped by two cultures: one foot in the traditions of his ancestors, the other in the intellectual circles of Rome. Though only in his early thirties, Tertius had already spent years among the educated, listening to discussions on law, philosophy, and politics, setting the words of others to parchment with the precision of a man trained in the art of language.

He bowed his head respectfully, gripping the scroll a little tighter. Confidence and apprehension warred within him.

Even in the silence, Paul's presence filled the room. His name was spoken with equal parts fear and reverence—a man who had once shaken the church with ruthless persecution,[1] then turned the world upside down through his radical conversion.[2] He had stormed through cities proclaiming the message he once sought to destroy,[3] his words igniting revival and riot in equal measure. Paul's reputation had spread across the empire, from Jerusalem to Rome, and now here he stood, in the flesh.

Tertius knew he was in the presence of greatness. What he did not yet understand was that he was about to become part of it.

"It's an honor to meet you, sir," Tertius said, his voice calm, though the glint of excitement in his eyes gave him away.

Paul studied him for a moment, a smile playing at the corners of his mouth. Yes, this one had potential. "I've heard good things about you, Tertius. Gaius speaks highly of your skills."

Gaius chuckled, placing a reassuring hand on Tertius' shoulder. "He's more than just skilled; he's eager to learn. I thought this would be a good opportunity for him—not just to assist you but to broaden his understanding of the gospel."

"Well," Paul said slowly, "the work ahead won't be easy. But if he's willing, he'll learn a great deal." His gaze returned to Tertius, studying him carefully. "Are you ready?"

Tertius straightened. "Yes, sir."

Gaius nodded approvingly and stepped back toward the door. "I'll leave you to it then. May the Lord guide you." He paused, casting one last glance at Paul before slipping out of the room, leaving them alone.

Tertius looked down, his heart thumping against his ribs. He moved quickly to the table in the center of the room, almost stumbling, but he caught himself.

With the practiced hands of a scribe, he set out his tools—reed pens, ink, parchment—each placed carefully on the table's worn surface.[4] He hesitated, then nudged the table to catch the sunlight streaming through the window.

Satisfied, he sat, back straightening, hands steady. The room seemed to pulsate with quiet intensity.

Paul watched, a spark of approval crossing his face. Without a word, he grabbed the chair he'd just been sitting in—the one by the table under the window—and dragged it closer, the legs scraping against the stone floor like a drawn-out sigh. He propped one foot on the seat, leaning forward, his eyes narrowing, thoughts sharpening like the point of the reed pen.

"Tertius, I have to warn you—this letter will be unlike any you've written before. It's a message to the churches I founded in the province of Galatia, and they are in grave danger. Their very souls are at risk."

Tertius looked up, concern and curiosity apparent in his eyes. He hesitated, the sensitivity of the subject demanding discretion and tact. "I…I've heard some of the rumors. Gaius and I talked about it earlier. He said that some people are stirring up trouble, trying to convince the Galatian believers they need to follow the

Law of Moses." He paused, his fingers nervously fidgeting with the pen. "Is it as bad as it sounds?"

Paul nodded, his expression turning grave. "Yes. Unfortunately, it is. That's why we must be clear and uncompromising. No room for pleasantries here. No long introductions, no extended blessings. We'll start with a quick introduction and then get straight to the heart of the matter."[5]

Tertius swallowed hard. "Yes, sir," he said, as he gripped the pen, ready for Paul's words.

A thick silence settled over the room. Paul turned his gaze to the simple cross hanging above the hearth. He let out a slow breath and then glanced back at Tertius. "Before we begin, let's pray," he said quietly.

Tertius nodded, bowing his head. Paul closed his eyes. The lines on his face seemed to soften as he began.

"Blessed are You, Lord God of our fathers," Paul murmured, his voice low, steady as the distant waves. "Grant me boldness to speak the truth plainly, with wisdom and love. May no man turn away from the path of righteousness. Pierce through the lies and call the Galatians back to freedom. And Lord, use this letter to silence the voices of those who proclaim a false gospel, and grant accuracy and speed to the pen of Your scribe, chosen by You for this holy purpose."

The air seemed to thicken with the power of Paul's prayer—as though they were standing before the very throne of God.

"Through Christ our Lord, amen," Paul finished, his voice fading like the last notes of a hymn.

Tertius lifted his head. The prayer had quieted the storm of uncertainty within him, grounding his spirit.

Paul opened his eyes and looked at him, a flash of determination in his gaze. "Now let's begin."

CHAPTER 2

THE HEART OF THE CONFLICT

(GALATIANS 1:1–5)

PAUL TOOK A deep breath and started dictating: **"This letter is from Paul, an apostle. I was not appointed by any group of people or any human authority, but by Jesus Christ himself and by God the Father, who raised Jesus from the dead"** (1:1).[1]

Paul's voice held a tension that cut through the air, every word weighted with meaning. The Judaizers had challenged not only his message but his very authority as an apostle. Perhaps they assumed that since he was not one of the Twelve, he carried less credibility—an outsider, a self-appointed teacher with no true mandate. They whispered their doubts in Galatia, questioning his right to speak for Christ, casting shadows over his gospel.

Paul knew he had to set the record straight before anything else. From the very first line, he made it clear—he was no mere envoy of men, but an apostle sent by Jesus Christ Himself.[2]

"All the brothers and sisters here join me in sending this letter to the churches of Galatia" (1:2), he continued.

The pen scratched the parchment, filling the room with its rhythm. Paul's thoughts drifted to the towns in southern Galatia—Pisidian Antioch, Iconium, Lystra, Derbe. Not grand cities but frontier towns on the edge of Roman order, where East met West and cultures clashed.[3]

In Iconium, they sacrificed to Zeus in the shadow of his temple. In Lystra, Hermes got the reverence. In city after city, temples loomed over the streets. Golden idols glistened, stone statues with lifeless eyes overseeing the crowds. Men and women prayed to gods of war, fertility, trade—pleading for rain, harvests, a loved one's safe return. The markets reeked of incense and the cries of animals offered to demons.

It was a world of offerings and omens, festivals that blurred revelry and reverence. Life—business, politics, marriage—hinged on the whims of these gods. The temples were at the heart of it all, priests guarding the gates to favor. Promises whispered in the dark, rituals meant to twist fate.

The synagogues stood in stark contrast, small but stubborn. Jewish families had lived here for generations, their lives shaped by the Torah, their hearts anchored by belief in one God. While the Gentiles burned incense to a pantheon of deities, the Jews worshipped Yahweh—unseen, unshaken, unchanging. No carved images. No statues in temples. No sacrifices to lifeless idols.

Their God spoke not through oracles but through prophets and sacred scrolls. His law was etched in stone. His people were set apart—not by wealth or power but by obedience. They kept the feasts. They observed the fasts. And for every Jewish man, a mark in his own flesh bore witness to the covenant. Circumcision—the sign that they belonged to Yahweh.

Two worlds, side by side. One with countless gods, the other with unshakable faith in one. And into this tension came the gospel, turning both worlds upside down.

The Gentiles scoffed—what kind of god lowers himself to be beaten, humiliated, and nailed to a cross? Gods demanded sacrifices; they didn't *become* them. The very idea was laughable, offensive even.

The Jews were even more challenged. The Messiah had come but not as they expected. He didn't march in with an army. He didn't overthrow Rome. He brought no sword, no rebellion—only a cross and an empty tomb. And with Him, a new covenant. One that said righteousness wasn't earned through the Law of Moses. Circumcision couldn't save. Sacrifices couldn't cleanse. Only faith in Jesus could.

And that, right there, was the heart of the conflict.

The Gentiles who embraced Paul's message turned away from idols, leaving behind the rituals that had trapped them in fear. No more offerings to imaginary beings, no more endless sacrifices. They found freedom in Christ—freedom from fear, from striving, from superstition. And it was glorious.

But now others had come. Men from Jerusalem, saying that faith in Christ wasn't enough. They had to follow the Law of Moses: circumcision, dietary laws, Sabbaths. The same rules that had always divided Jew and Gentile. To Paul, these men—the Judaizers—weren't just flawed teachers. They were a threat to the gospel itself.

The room was quiet. Paul broke the silence.

"Before I drop the hammer," he said, his voice calm but firm, "let me first say something gracious to my brothers and sisters and give glory to the Lord."

He cleared his throat, eyes narrowing with focus. **"May God the Father and our Lord Jesus Christ give you grace and peace. Jesus gave his life for our sins, just as God our Father planned, in order to rescue us from this evil world in which we live" (1:3–4).**[4]

Closing his eyes, Paul lifted his head, arms spreading wide in worship.

"All glory to God forever and ever! Amen" (1:5).

CHAPTER 3

THE CURSE

(GALATIANS 1:6–9)

WITHOUT TURNING, PAUL continued, his voice punching low and hard. "Write this: **'I am shocked that you are turning away so soon from God, who called you to himself through the loving mercy of Christ'**" (1:6).

Tertius began writing, his reed pen scratching across the parchment.

A frown crossed Paul's face. "A different way," he muttered to himself, as though still processing the absurdity of it.

"Write this: **'You are following a different way that pretends to be the Good News'**" (1:6).[1] His voice rose, each word punctuated with urgency, almost pleading: **"...but is not the Good News at all. You are being fooled by those who deliberately twist the truth concerning Christ"** (1:7).

Tertius scribed the words dutifully, but his brow knit in confusion. "Are you saying they're twisting the gospel on purpose?"

Paul looked up, his expression sharp. "Of course they are, Tertius. What did you think was going on?"

"I assumed these men were sincere, just...misinformed."

Paul exhaled, shaking his head. "Oh, I'm sure they think they're right. Everyone thinks they're right—even the pagans and idolaters. I did too, when I hunted down believers in the name of God. I was sincere. And I was dead wrong."

He leaned forward, his voice lowering.

"But this is different, Tertius. I was blind—I didn't know who Jesus was. I fought the gospel in ignorance. But these men? They've heard the truth. They've claimed to believe it. And now, they're twisting it—not from the *outside* but from within. They're not just lost; they're leading others off the path, using the name of Christ to do it."

The words hung heavy in the room. Paul exhaled sharply, then started to pace.

Tertius' brow furrowed. "But there is some truth in what they're saying, right?"

Paul shook his head, his jaw clenched. "That's the worst part, Tertius. There *is* truth in it—but it's twisted. The most dangerous lies are the ones that have just enough truth in them."

Tertius sat back, trying to absorb everything Paul was saying.

"I mean," Paul continued, "if these false teachers had come in preaching some weird pagan nonsense, the Galatians would've shut them down right away. But because they wrapped their lies in the clothes of the gospel, they got a foot in the door."

A shadow crossed Tertius' face as the depth of the threat became clearer. "So they used the credibility of Scripture to back their lies."

Paul's countenance darkened, his voice dropping to a near growl. "You got it. Like the Greeks hiding inside the Trojan Horse. The Galatians opened the gates, thinking it was a gift, but they've let in their own destruction."

Paul's expression grew distant, as if he could see the faces of those he had preached to—faces now shadowed by doubt and deception.

"These teachers," he began again, his voice roughened by anger, "they follow me from town to town like a plague, spreading lies, twisting the truth, and leading new believers away from the simplicity of Christ."

Tertius nodded, reed pen poised over parchment. "Gaius told me about them," he admitted cautiously. "He said they're persuasive, highly educated men, full-blooded Jews. Some are even quite well known in Jerusalem itself."

"I don't care if they're the archangels Michael and Gabriel," Paul growled, his voice low and fierce. "In fact, write this: **'Let God's curse fall on anyone, including us or even an angel from heaven, who preaches a different kind of Good News than the one we preached to you. I say again what we have said before:**[2] **"If anyone preaches any other Good News than the one you welcomed, let that person be cursed"'"** (1:8–9).

"Wow. That's…intense, sir."

Paul paused, glancing over his shoulder. His expression softened, if only for a fleeting moment. "It *is* intense, Tertius," he replied, turning fully to face him. "But it must be."

Tertius hesitated, the pen hovering uncertainly above the parchment. "But why a curse, sir? Why go that far?"

"Because it's exactly what these teachers are using to deceive the Galatians. They whisper that my gospel puts them under a curse, that without the law they are condemned."

His jaw tightened, his eyes burning with frustration. "But they don't understand the true nature of the curse. They hold up the law as if it could break sin's power. But the law never removed the curse—it only revealed it. The real curse—the first curse—fell on humanity long before the law ever existed."

Paul leaned forward. "Think back, Tertius. To the beginning. To the garden. Adam and Eve's sin brought death—not just as a punishment but as a curse on all creation. That was the moment everything fractured. And what did they do when they realized they had sinned?"

Tertius nodded, his eyes drifting off into the distance as he pictured the familiar tale.

"They hid!"[3] he blurted out, a little too loudly. "They tried to cover themselves with fig leaves to hide their nakedness because they couldn't bear the shame."

A brief silence followed. Tertius blinked, suddenly aware he may have sounded like an overeager schoolboy.

"That's right." Paul smiled, clearly amused by Tertius' enthusiasm. "They thought they could cover their shame with their own efforts. But tell me, what did God do?"

Tertius closed his eyes, the scene unfolding in vivid detail within his mind. The pieces of a puzzle clicking into place. "God…He clothed them…with animal skins."[4]

"Yes!" Paul exclaimed. "The fig leaves were Adam and Eve's way of trying to fix their mistake—something they made with their own hands to cover their shame. But God rejected these fig leaf coverings and gave them animal skins instead, which meant an innocent animal had to die."

Paul leaned forward, his gaze locked onto Tertius, his words clear and deliberate, each one a hammer striking the nail.

"Think of it this way—God rejected the work of their hands…

He covered their shame…

With the ultimate sacrifice…

Of an innocent substitute."

Tertius sank back in his chair. His eyes widened, the connection illuminating his mind.

"There was nothing Adam and Eve could do to cover their shame," Paul continued. "God had to provide the answer, and it required blood, sacrifice—substitution.

"That's what our entire sacrificial system points to. That's why every morning and evening a lamb was slain in the Temple. Every year at Passover, families brought a spotless lamb to be sacrificed. Blood had to be spilled, day after day, year after year. The priests kept slaughtering. The altar never rested—because it could never truly remove sin, only cover it for a time."

He let the thought breathe before speaking again.

"But Tertius, think back. What did John the Baptist say when he first saw Jesus?"

Tertius blinked, his thoughts racing, piecing together fragments of teachings and stories. The realization struck him, and he exhaled the words with reverence.

"Behold the Lamb of God, who takes away the sin of the world."[5]

Tertius' eyes remained wide, his mouth slightly open, as though the enormity of the truth had struck him physically, leaving him dazed.

Paul leaned forward, his gaze piercing. "God took the One who had never sinned and placed all our sin upon Him so that, in return, we could be made right with God through Him. God has provided for us ultimate righteousness, provided by the ultimate sacrifice of the ultimate innocent substitute.

"But without the cross," Paul continued, "there is no remedy—no covering for sin. A man outside of Christ is under the curse by default—the wrath of God remains on him.[6] So you see, I'm not the one doing the cursing, Tertius. Without Christ, they're cursed already."

"This is...heavy, sir," Tertius murmured. "The Galatians need to hear this."

"They will," Paul replied, turning to the window. "That's why we're writing."

CHAPTER 4

FIG LEAVES

(GALATIANS 1:10)

PAUL REACHED UNDER the table to the leather sack that lay there, heavy and waiting. He opened it carefully and tilted it just enough to let the contents tumble onto the table. A soft clunking filled the room as seven pottery shards spilled out, their reddish-brown surfaces catching the sunlight streaming through the window. Each piece bore marks of intricate design—a few painted with faded patterns of yellow wildflowers, remnants of a former beauty.

Setting the sack aside, Paul reached out, turning the shards over one by one, revealing their matte, scratched interiors. There in the morning light, lines of writing emerged—notes he had scribbled to himself with the fine strokes of a stylus.

Each piece bore a headline, a starting point for thought. From these, lines of simple text branched out, intricate and winding. One- or two-word prompts mapped out numerous theological arguments and musings. It was a puzzle, each fragment of clay revealing a glimpse into the vast maze of Paul's mind.[1]

These weren't the usual flat, plain pottery shards normally used for note-taking. No, these pieces came from an ornate amphora,[2] painted with delicate patterns, crafted with rare artistry. Each broken fragment curved gracefully, hinting at the original form.

Tertius leaned in, eyes floating over the pieces. "These are beautiful," he whispered. "Where did they come from?"

Paul met Tertius' gaze, his expression distant. "There's a story there, Tertius," he said softly, voice laden with unspoken memories. "But now is not the time. We have work to do."

Tertius straightened, recognizing something unspoken in Paul's tone. Turning his attention away from the shards, he sensed another question pressing at the edges of his mind, one he had long wanted to ask. Now, it seemed, might be the moment.

"Sir, may I ask you something?" He shifted in his seat, his discomfort evident in the way he avoided Paul's gaze.

Paul raised an eyebrow, intrigued. "Go on."

Tertius cleared his throat, stealing a quick glance at Paul's face before looking away again.

"There are those who say you're against circumcision—that you're teaching people to abandon our traditions. Is that true?"

Paul was silent for a moment, studying his young scribe. There was no accusation in his voice, only a desire to understand.

When Paul finally spoke, his voice was steady, full of care. "I've heard those rumors, too, Tertius, and they've got it wrong. I'm not against circumcision—it was the sign of God's covenant with Abraham. The problem comes when people think circumcision—or any part of the law—makes them right with God. That's where they miss it."

Paul leaned back slightly. "In fact, I had a Gentile named Timothy circumcised a few months ago."[3]

Tertius blinked in surprise.

"His mother is Jewish, but his father is Greek. His father refused to have him circumcised at birth. So I had him circumcised—but not because it made him closer to God or gave him special favor."

Tertius tilted his head. "Then why?"

Paul exhaled. "Because the Jews in the area *knew* his father was Greek. They would have asked if he was circumcised before allowing him into their homes or their meetings. If he couldn't say yes, doors would have been shut—to him, to us, and to the gospel."

Tertius nodded, a new understanding dawning. "So it's not circumcision itself that's the issue—it's the belief that it's required for salvation?"

"It's more than that," Paul clarified. "We brought this before the leaders in Jerusalem, and they agreed—circumcision isn't required for salvation. But the Judaizers have found a loophole. Now they claim Gentiles *can* be saved by faith, but to *fully* belong—to be counted as true heirs of Abraham's blessing—they must be circumcised. That's how they twist the truth.

"Many Jews already believed that while some Gentiles could be saved, they would always be second-class—outsiders spared from judgment but never true children of God. The Judaizers are distorting what was settled in Jerusalem, turning it into something it was never meant to be. But their version is just as dangerous as the other. And I intend to make that very clear in this letter."

Paul's eyes darkened with conviction. "If anyone—Jew or Gentile—believes an outward act like circumcision makes them more acceptable to God, they're rejecting what Christ did for us. It's like saying the cross wasn't enough."

A slow nod came from Tertius, satisfied by Paul's response. "That seems simple enough. So why is circumcision still so appealing to the Galatians? You'd think they'd be glad to avoid something so painful."

Paul's expression tightened as he weighed his response. "It's more than just theology, Tertius. For a lot of people, circumcision offers status—validation. It gives them a sense that they're finally crossing over from outsider to insider."

Tertius raised an eyebrow. "Status?"

Paul nodded. "Absolutely. See, a lot of the Gentile believers already had a deep respect for God long before they heard about Christ. They were what we call *God-fearers*—Gentiles who rejected paganism and worshipped the God of Israel. They attended synagogue, studied the Scriptures, even observed the Sabbath and dietary laws. But there was always a line they couldn't cross."[4]

He leaned forward, his voice steady. "No matter how devoted they were, they were still outsiders. If they wanted to be fully accepted—if they wanted to truly belong—they had to go all the way. And that meant circumcision. That was the dividing line. Some of them took that step, but most couldn't bring themselves to do it."

A small smile tugged at the corner of Paul's mouth. "Then they heard the gospel. The message of Jesus turned their world upside down. For the first time, they were told that through His shed blood they could be fully included—no circumcision, no Mosaic Law, nothing but faith in Christ. The door that had always been cracked open was now thrown wide. Those who were once far away had been brought near. And they were overjoyed."

He gestured toward the open window, as if picturing the distant congregations. "And what a glorious time it was. These new believers—freed from guilt, fear, and endless striving—flourished in their faith. Entire communities sprang to life. Jew and Gentile broke bread together, worshipped side by side, called one another family. The Spirit moved among them, filling their gatherings with power, transforming their lives. They were not just accepted—they were alive. And the world took notice."

Paul's expression darkened. "But then the whispers started. The doubts crept in. The Judaizers came, pulling them aside, telling them, 'What Jesus did for you is incredible—truly, it is. Faith in Him is good. But imagine how much better it would be if you were also a Jew. That's the higher status, the elite level. You're so close—almost there. Just take that next step and you'll really belong. You'll be the real deal—a true child of Abraham.'"

Tertius leaned back, his brow furrowed as he let the words sink in. "So they're preying on their desire to be seen as fully legitimate—not just in God's eyes but in the eyes of the community."

Paul pointed at him. "Exactly! It plays on their deepest longing—to be fully accepted, fully included. No more second-class status. No more standing at the edge of the synagogue, looking in. Just one little step and they can seal the deal."

Tertius shook his head. "That's insidious."

"And it doesn't stop there." Paul continued, "Circumcision gives them a sense of safety too. They figure that by becoming full Jewish converts, they'll belong to a bigger, more well-known community under the umbrella of Judaism. For a lot of them, it feels safer to stick with something more mainstream, something established and recognized, than to follow Christ and end up separated from everybody—Jews and pagans alike."

Tertius nodded slowly, his mind piecing together the complex emotions at play. "So it's both status *and* safety."

Paul sighed. "Yes, but it's more than that. Circumcision also gives them a sense of self-righteousness—which might be the most dangerous trap of all."

"What's wrong with being self-righteous?"

Paul fixed his eyes on Tertius. "People have this urge to fix their own sin. Think back to what we said about Adam and Eve in the garden. The second they felt shame, what did they do? They grabbed fig leaves and covered up their nakedness—the work of their own hands."

Tertius waited for Paul to go on.

"But remember what God did?" Paul said. "He rejected their fig-leaf coverings and clothed them with the skin of animals—innocent victims who paid the ultimate price. You see, Adam and Eve underestimated their sin problem. It wasn't something that a few strategically placed leaves could fix. Something, *someone*, had to die."

Tertius' mind raced through the Scriptures—images of the Passover lamb's blood on the doorframes, sin offerings with blood sprinkled for cleansing, and the solemn rites of the Day of Atonement. The law was clear: "The soul that sins shall die."[5] The penalty was death, and there was no avoiding it.

But then he recalled another truth—the mercy of substitution: "The life of the flesh is in the blood, and I have given it for you on the altar to make atonement for your souls."[6]

From the beginning God had made it clear: Sin required death, but in His mercy, He provided a sacrifice—a life given in place of the sinner. And now, as Paul spoke, Tertius saw it with fresh eyes. Circumcision, like fig leaves, could never cover their guilt. Only blood could. Only Christ could.

Paul leaned in. "Circumcision, Tertius, is no different from those fig leaves in the garden—just a covering, a work of human hands trying to fix what only God can. If the law could make us right, why did Jesus have to die?"[7]

His voice rose with conviction. "Jesus doesn't just *cover* our sin—He *clothes* us in His righteousness."

Tertius smiled with admiration. "I can see how much this matters to you, sir. But what if the Judaizers accuse you of giving the Gentiles an easy path to salvation, just to get popular?"

Paul gave a short, incredulous laugh. "Ha! Really? If I were out to please people, would I be shouting things like, 'Let anyone preaching another gospel be cursed'? Do you think that's the kind of message that wins folks over?"

Tertius' pen stilled in his hand, the sharpness of Paul's response catching him off guard. "No, I suppose not," he murmured.

Paul's eyes burned with a fire that left no room for doubt. "If I wanted to be popular, I'd have stayed a Pharisee. I had it all—status, respect, influence. I followed the law to the letter, and the religious leaders loved me for it. I gave all that up to become a servant of Christ."

He looked directly at Tertius. "Now write this: **'Obviously, I'm not trying to win the approval of people, but of God. If pleasing people were my goal, I would not be Christ's servant'**" (1:10).

As Tertius dipped his pen and began to scratch the words onto the parchment, Paul's intensity seemed to ebb, folding inward.

His fingers twitched slightly—a faint, unconscious motion—then drifted to his side, tracing the edge of something hidden. He winced as he touched it.

Tertius kept writing, eyes down, pretending not to notice, but in that unguarded moment, he understood: Paul's gospel was more than arguments and doctrine. He bore deep scars and had paid a profound price to follow Jesus.

CHAPTER 5

DAMASCUS ROAD

(GALATIANS 1:11–17)

PAUL TURNED FROM the window, his voice steady. "Tertius, this is the perfect time to remind the Galatians of my story. They've heard it before—probably know it by heart—but it needs repeating.

"The Judaizers are twisting things, making it sound as if I got my message from the apostles in Jerusalem. If that were true, they could tell me to change it. But it's not. I didn't learn this from any man—I received it straight from Jesus. And the Galatians need to hear that loud and clear."

Tertius straightened, readying his reed pen once more.

"Start with this," Paul said. **"Dear brothers and sisters, I want you to understand that the gospel message I preach is not based on mere human reasoning"** (1:11).

Tertius' hand moved quickly across the parchment.

Paul continued, pacing as he spoke. **"I received my message from no human source, and no one taught me. Instead, I received it by direct revelation from Jesus Christ"** (1:12).

Tertius paused, glancing up at Paul with uncertainty in his eyes. "Uh, sir, don't you think that might be saying the same thing twice? I mean…if you received your message directly from Jesus, then isn't it already clear it didn't come from any man?"

Paul stopped and cast a quick glance at the parchment. "Good catch, Tertius. You've got the instincts of a careful scribe."

Tertius straightened a little, allowing himself a flicker of pride.

"But this is precisely what I need to say," Paul blurted.

Tertius blinked, clearly thrown off.

Paul continued. "I need to make two points. First, this gospel I preach does not come from Jerusalem and the leaders there; in fact, it comes from no human source at all. Second, if it does not come from man, then where does it come from? I need to stress that it comes from Jesus Himself. That is why it is wrongheaded to think I need approval from any man before I can preach my message."

Paul paced for a moment. "First, let's remind them of the story: **'You know what I was like when I followed the Jewish religion—how I violently persecuted God's church. I did my best to destroy it. I was far ahead of my fellow Jews in my zeal for the traditions of my ancestors'**" (1:13–14).

Tertius' reed pen scratched across the parchment as he carefully transcribed Paul's words, but curiosity gnawed at him. He looked up, hesitant. "Sir…I know the Galatians have heard the story before, but I haven't. Would you tell me what happened?"

"Well, it's a long story, so I'll give you the short version. You know I wasn't always known as Paul, right? Among my people, I used to go by Saul. I was born into a proud Jewish family from the tribe of Benjamin. Tarsus was my hometown."

Tertius nodded with recognition. "That's in the east, isn't it?"

"Yes. Beyond the sea, past Cyprus, just south of the Cilician Gates—the great mountain pass where all the commerce flows east and west. A strategic city—prosperous, full of bustling streets and markets, merchants from all over, and no shortage of Roman and Greek influence.[1] My family were landowners there, Roman citizens too."

Paul caught Tertius' look. He didn't need to say more; Tertius knew. Roman citizenship was a rare privilege, especially by birth.

"At fourteen," Paul continued, "I was chosen—handpicked really—to study under Gamaliel."

"Gamaliel?" Tertius said, his eyes wide. "You mean *the* Gamaliel?"

"That's the one. The grandson of Hillel the Elder," Paul confirmed, a knowing look in his eyes. He could see the change in Tertius' expression, the awe and respect that settled there. Gamaliel and Shammai were the two greatest teachers in Judaism at the time. To be chosen by one of them was as prestigious a laurel as any in the Jewish religious world.

Paul paused, his face hardening as he recalled the zeal of his younger self. "But I wasn't just a student. I became a Pharisee—one of the most zealous, fiery followers of the law. I was determined to silence anything that threatened our sacred traditions. Especially those followers of the Way. We called them a 'sect'—worshipping a man crucified like a common criminal and claiming he'd risen from the dead. To me, it was pure blasphemy. But what bothered me even more was how it spread among our own people. The message caught like wildfire, and I made it my life's mission to stamp it out."

The room grew colder as he spoke. "The name 'Saul of Tarsus' struck fear in the hearts of believers. I hunted them down, dragged them out of their homes, and threw them in prison. I truly thought I was fighting for God, standing up for the truth."[2]

Tertius listened, eyes wide, stunned by the ferocity in Paul's recounting. He had known bits and pieces of the story, but never like this.

"Then came Stephen," Paul said, his tone softening. "He was the first."

His eyes grew distant, as if staring into the past. "I'll never forget that day. It was scorching—one of those blistering afternoons in Jerusalem. The crowd had him cornered, faces twisted with rage, stones already clutched in their hands. I was there, standing off to the side, holding their cloaks so they'd be free to do the job."

He paused, the memory playing out in his mind like a dark scene.

"Stephen wasn't afraid. Not even when they dragged him into the open, his clothes ripping on the stones. He had this strange calm about him, eyes fixed on something the rest of us couldn't see. They circled him like wolves, shouting, spitting, calling him a blasphemer. And then the first stone flew."

Paul's jaw tightened, his voice dropping as he recalled the details.

"I watched every bit of it, every strike, every blow. Stones rained down, one after another, and still he stood there, battered but upright. His face, Tertius—it shone like he was staring straight into the face of God.[3] Blood ran down his forehead, but he didn't scream. Instead, he looked up, right past us, into the sky."[4] I'll never forget his words. 'Look,' he said, 'I see heaven opened and the Son of Man standing at the right hand of God.'[5] The crowd roared, fury spilling over, but I felt this…chill run down my spine. It didn't make sense to me back then, but I couldn't look away."

Paul let out a sharp breath, as if he'd been holding it for years. "But those weren't the most amazing words he spoke. Stephen fell to his knees as the stones kept coming, and I heard him shout, 'Lord, do not hold this sin against them.'[6] It cut through me like a knife.

"People being executed usually curse their accusers. This was the first time I heard of someone asking God to forgive them. I found out later he was just following in the footsteps of his Master. Jesus, I am told, did the same thing when He was hanging on the cross.[7] But at the time, I didn't know any of that. I just stood there, nodding in approval of what they were doing, but inside I was confused. This man had something I didn't have."

Paul straightened, his eyes sharpening. "But I didn't let

it bother me for long. I *couldn't*. Instead, I threw myself even harder into the cause. I buried the doubt, silenced the questions, and redoubled my efforts to put an end to this movement. If Stephen's words had rattled me, I would crush them with action. That's why, right after he died, I went straight to the high priest and demanded permission to hunt down these 'followers of the Way' all the way to Damascus. I was relentless. I was burning with anger. I *needed* to prove I was right. But on the road… everything changed."[8]

Paul's voice dropped to almost a whisper. "As I was getting close to Damascus, a light from heaven flashed down all around me, brighter than the sun. It knocked me flat on the ground."

Tertius' eyes locked on Paul's intense expression; he was hanging on every word.

"And then I heard a voice, Tertius. It said, 'Saul, Saul, why are you persecuting Me?'"

Paul's gaze drifted, his expression distant, as if he were back on that dusty road. "I asked, 'Who are You, Lord?' And the voice answered, 'I am Jesus, the One you're persecuting.'"

His breath caught for a moment. When he spoke again, his voice was quavering. "In that instant, everything I thought I knew—everything I had built my life on—collapsed. I wasn't fighting *for* God…" He hesitated, the words catching in his throat. "I was fighting *against* Him."

A stunned silence filled the room, the weight of Paul's confession settling heavily between them.

"I was struck blind," Paul continued. "For three days, I couldn't see a thing. They had to guide me into Damascus, and I waited. Then God sent a man named Ananias to me. He laid his hands on me, and my sight was restored. It was like scales falling from my eyes. That's when I knew…I wasn't Saul the Pharisee anymore. From that moment on, I became Saul, a servant of Christ."[9]

Tertius exhaled slowly, fascinated by the story. "So that's when you received the revelation of the gospel?"

Paul smiled softly. "No, Tertius. That's when I received the revelation of Jesus. In fact, let's write that.

"But even before I was born, God chose me and called me by his marvelous grace. Then it pleased him to reveal his Son to me so that I would proclaim the Good News about Jesus to the Gentiles. When this happened, I did not rush out to consult with any human being. Nor did I go up to Jerusalem to consult with those who were apostles before I was. Instead, I went away into Arabia, and later I returned to the city of Damascus" (1:15–17).

CHAPTER 6

ARABIA

PAUL PAUSED, ALLOWING Tertius a moment to catch up, his pacing filling the small room with an undercurrent of restless energy. His hands were clasped tightly behind his back, and Tertius noticed a subtle change in Paul's demeanor. It was as though there was something unsaid, something buried beneath the surface of his words.

Tertius glanced up from the parchment, his fingers pausing on the page as he reread the last line. "Sir, if you don't mind me asking…you said that before you returned to Damascus, you went away into Arabia. Why did you go there?"

Paul stopped mid-stride, a trace of a smile crossing his face.

"Tell me, Tertius, when you hear the word *Arabia*, what comes to mind?"

Tertius frowned slightly, considering. "Arabia? Well…the Nabateans,[1] the great cities of Petra and Bostra, the vast trade routes. It's mostly wilderness, isn't it? Dangerous roads, nomadic tribes, long stretches of nothing but sand and rock."

Paul turned fully to face him, his voice patient but insistent. "But there's something else, Tertius…a place. Something central to our faith, especially to the giving of the law."

Suddenly Tertius' eyes widened. "Mount Sinai!" He pointed at Paul, excitement in his voice. "That's where the law was given. That's where Moses saw the glory of God!"

Paul nodded, resuming his pacing, though his steps had slowed. His voice lowered, taking on a reverent tone.

"That's right. After my encounter with the Lord on the Damascus Road, my head was spinning. My heart was in turmoil. Everything I'd ever believed—everything I'd lived for—was flipped upside down in an instant. I didn't need to consult any scribe or scholar. I didn't even need the apostles. I needed God. I needed to make sense of what had just happened to me."

Tertius could feel the intensity building, his own heart thumping as he watched Paul, carried along by the story.

"For weeks I couldn't sleep," Paul continued, as if he were talking to himself more than to Tertius. "Early one morning, before the sun had even peeked over the horizon, I packed just the essentials—enough for the journey. I had to go to the place where Moses received the law, where God's glory came down like fire on the mountain. I had to go there, to the very heart of it all."[2]

His gaze drifted, his thoughts lost in the memory. "The closer I got, the more desolate the land became. Nothing but stretches of arid wasteland, twisted shrubs, sand, rocks. The wind howled, throwing stinging sand at me. I covered my head with my cloak and pushed on, driven by a deep sense of desperation. And then suddenly there it was..."

Paul paused, lifting his hand as though reaching for something unseen, his eyes looking into the distance.

"Imagine it, Tertius. That mountain," Paul said, his voice filled with awe. "The place where the air crackled with the power of God's presence. Storm clouds gathering, the voice of God thundering like a trumpet blast. The mountain so holy that if anyone touched it—even an animal—they'd be stoned to death. It's where Moses trembled in fear."[3]

He paused, his voice thick with emotion. "And I went there. I threw myself down in that place, crying out, 'O God of my fathers! Reveal Yourself to me!'"[4]

The room fell silent for a tense moment.

"That's where I saw it."

"Saw what, sir?" Tertius swallowed hard, clinging to every word as if the next might hold the answer to everything.

Paul's voice dropped to a whisper, his gaze unfocused, struggling for the right words.

"Greater glory."

Tertius barely dared to breathe.

"I can't put it into words, not completely," Paul said, shaking his head as if to brush away the limitations of language. "I don't even know how long I was there. The days blurred together. I only know that when I left, I wasn't the same man who arrived."

Tertius blinked, struggling to grasp the magnitude of what Paul was describing.

"When I saw it—when I saw Him," Paul continued, his voice charged with emotion, "everything I'd ever learned, every tradition I'd clung to, every achievement I was proud of…it all faded away. It was trash, dung even, compared to the reality of Christ."[5]

Tertius watched Paul intently. He sensed there was more, something deeper in Paul's words, a revelation that hovered just out of reach.

"Anyway," Paul said, his voice lower now, "when I say I didn't receive this gospel from any human, that's exactly what I mean. Jesus gave it to me personally. But I can't tell you everything that happened. Some things…they can't be put into words.[6] They're too astounding, too…" He trailed off.

Tertius looked up, eyes squinting. "Too what, sir?"

Paul's expression remained distant, seeing something far beyond the confines of their small room. "Did you write down that 'I received it by direct revelation from Jesus Christ'?"

"Yes, sir. I wrote it already," Tertius replied, curiosity sparking within him, but he knew better than to push for more.

Paul's eyes refocused, a small sigh slipping from his lips, as if he were returning from another world. "Good. That's all they need to know."

CHAPTER 7

THE TURNAROUND

(GALATIANS 1:18–24)

TERTIUS NOTICED THE subtle twitch of Paul's fingers, a fleeting sign that something unspoken still lingered. But Paul quickly turned back to the task at hand, pushing the moment aside.

"Let's continue. Write, **'Then three years later I went to Jerusalem to get to know Peter, and I stayed with him for fifteen days. The only other apostle I met at that time was James, the Lord's brother. I declare before God that what I am writing to you is not a lie**'" (1:18–20).

Tertius wrote, then paused, reed pen suspended. Paul's tone had changed, grave and solemn. "I declare before God" rang out, more oath than statement, echoing the prophets of old. Paul wasn't just stating a fact but swearing on his own integrity, calling God as his witness. Bold and risky, it invited divine judgment if false.[1]

"That's...strong language, sir," Tertius muttered. "Swearing an oath like that—before God—it makes me wonder. No one bothers to say such a thing unless there's some real debate. But why would anyone think you'd lie about something as trivial as staying with Peter and James for a few days?"

Paul stopped pacing abruptly, his eyes snapping to Tertius with a fierceness that made the scribe's heart skip a beat. "Oh, there's a debate, all right! The Judaizers are claiming that everything I know about Jesus came straight from the apostles. They say I'm just repeating what I learned from Peter or James, twisting it to fit my own message."

Tertius tilted his head to one side. "But sir, if you want to make it clear that your gospel didn't come from Peter and James, why mention that you stayed with them in the first place?"

Paul frowned. "Because I *did* stay with Peter. I'm not denying that at all. But I was only with him for fifteen days. Fifteen days, Tertius! Not long enough to gather all the wisdom and insight I've been preaching for all these years. And I barely even saw James. When I met Peter and James, it wasn't to learn the gospel. It was to confirm what I already knew. What Jesus had already revealed to me."

Tertius hesitated. "But people in the church tell me that Jesus commanded us never to swear."[2]

Paul nodded. "It's true.[3] Jesus warned against careless oaths. You've seen how people use them—to make themselves sound believable, even when they don't mean it. 'I swear by heaven,' 'I swear by Jerusalem'—as if those oaths don't count the same as swearing by God. They treat these oaths like a loophole, a way to make a promise sound binding while keeping an escape route open. That's what Jesus condemned—not the kind of oath that confirms truth, but the kind that disguises deception.

"But when a witness in court takes an oath, it's to confirm the truth when it matters most. Even God swore an oath to Abraham—not because He needed to, but to remove any doubt. And what I'm saying here—it's of supreme importance. The agitators call me a liar, but I call heaven to witness. I stake everything on the truth of my testimony."

Tertius nodded, understanding dawning.

"They need to know, beyond a shadow of a doubt, that I did not get my revelation of the gospel from any man."

Paul's eyes suddenly lit up, as if a new thought had struck him out of the blue. "Write this: **'After that visit I went north into**

the provinces of Syria and Cilicia. And still the churches in Christ that are in Judea didn't know me personally'" (1:21–22).

Tertius looked up. "Why is that important, sir?"

Paul leaned forward, his eyes sharp. "Because it shows, yet again, that I couldn't have been coached or informed by the apostles. After those fifteen days with Peter, I didn't stay in Judea where they were. I went north, to Syria and Cilicia. I was in an entirely different province. I wasn't even in Judea long enough for the believers there to get to know me."

Tertius nodded slowly as he carefully transcribed Paul's words. "But I'm sure those believers in Judea knew *about* you, right, sir?"

A wry smile played at the corner of Paul's lips. "Oh, they knew about me, Tertius. They most certainly did. But not in the way you might think."

Tertius looked up from the parchment, curiosity flickering in his gaze.

Paul sat down in his chair, his voice tinged with irony and reflection. "They didn't know my face. They couldn't have picked me out of a crowd. But they knew my story. They'd heard the whispers—the tales of the one who used to hunt down and attack the church. Imagine their shock when they discovered I was now preaching the very faith I once tried to wipe out."

Paul's eyes gleamed with the power of the transformation. "And what was their reaction? They praised God because of me. Write it down, Tertius: **'All they knew was that people were saying, "The one who used to persecute us is now preaching the very faith he tried to destroy!" And they praised God because of me**'" (1:23–24).

Tertius smiled as he wrote the final line. "Quite the turnaround, sir."

CHAPTER 8

PIGS IN A BLANKET

(GALATIANS 2:1–4)

"READ THAT LAST line back to me, Tertius," Paul instructed.

Tertius quickly scanned the parchment before reading aloud, **"After that visit I went north into the provinces of Syria and Cilicia. And still the churches in Christ that are in Judea didn't know me personally. All they knew was that people were saying, 'The one who used to persecute us is now preaching the very faith he tried to destroy!' And they praised God because of me"** (1:21–24).

Paul nodded. "Yes. Let's keep moving."

Tertius dipped his reed pen, ready to continue as Paul's voice took on a sharper edge, diving back into the narrative.

"Then fourteen years later I went back to Jerusalem again, this time with Barnabas; and Titus came along, too. I went there because God revealed to me that I should go. While I was there I met privately with those considered to be leaders of the church and shared with them the message I had been preaching to the Gentiles. I wanted to make sure that we were in agreement, for fear that all my efforts had been wasted and I was running the race for nothing" (2:1–2).

Tertius raised an eyebrow as he wrote. "So you didn't return to Jerusalem again for fourteen years?"[1]

"Well, I did make a short visit a few years before that, but that was just to deliver an offering to the church during the famine. I did not see any apostles then, just some of the local church elders. That visit is not relevant to the point I'm making here, so we won't mention it."

Paul stood, reaching for a clay pitcher on the table. It was rough-hewn, the kind that had seen years of use, maybe generations. He poured water into two simple wooden cups, the liquid splashing softly in the quiet room. Handing one cup to Tertius, he took a quick drink from his own.

"Were you looking for validation?" Tertius said.

Paul shook his head. "Not exactly. The gospel I preach came directly from Jesus—I wasn't looking for their stamp of approval. But if their message had clashed with mine, that would've been a problem, a big one."

Tertius looked up, puzzled. "But why talk about running in vain? Were you afraid you might have been wrong?"

Paul let out a dry laugh—not of amusement but recognition. "No, not at all. I was afraid that if the apostles didn't stand with me, the mission could fall apart before it even got off the ground."

He leaned forward, resting both hands on the table. "Imagine what would've happened, Tertius—two gospels, two messages. Confusion. Division. And the Gentile believers we had already reached? They'd be the ones to suffer. Pulled back into law, torn between leaders, unsure of what to believe. Some might've fallen away completely. If that happened, it wouldn't matter how true my gospel was—the mission would be shipwrecked. That's what I meant by running in vain."

Tertius shifted in his seat. "Ahh…I see," he said quietly.

"But we were all on the same page. We shared the same gospel—it came from the same source, Jesus! Read that last line to me again."

"I wanted to make sure that we were in agreement, for fear that all my efforts had been wasted and I was running the race for nothing," Tertius recited.

"That's right," Paul said. **"And they supported me and did not even demand that my companion Titus be circumcised, though he was a Gentile. Even that question came up only because of some so-called believers there—false ones, really—who were secretly brought in. They sneaked in to spy on us and take away the freedom we have in Christ Jesus. They wanted to enslave us and force us to follow their Jewish regulations"** (2:3–4).

Tertius glanced up from the parchment. "Spies, sir?"

"Yes, spies," Paul responded tersely.

Tertius watched Paul carefully. "You seem agitated, sir."

Paul exhaled sharply, rubbing a hand across his face. "You know what, Tertius? We've been at this a while. Let's take a little break. I think some fresh air will do us good."

Tertius nodded in agreement, setting his reed pen aside. Paul stood up and stretched, feeling the tightness in his muscles. They stepped outside, letting the cool breeze wash over them—a welcome relief after the intensity of their work.

They walked for a while in silence, the countryside around them alive with quiet energy. The air was fragrant with wild herbs, and the earth beneath their sandals felt reassuringly solid, grounding them after the morning's intense focus.

It was Paul who broke the silence. "Let me tell you a story," he began, his voice dropping low, as though he were pulling the words from deep within. "I think you'll appreciate this one. It'll set the stage for what we need to write next."

Tertius glanced over, intrigued. Paul's stories weren't just stories—they were like a slow burn, starting soft then catching fire until you couldn't look away.

"This all happened about ten years ago, in Caesarea," Paul said. "Now, you know Caesarea, right? It's a Roman hub, bustling with soldiers and merchants, the air thick with the scent of spices and salt from the sea. In that city lived a man named Cornelius.[2] You couldn't miss him in a crowd—tall, broad-shouldered, with a presence that made soldiers snap to attention. A centurion, a leader of men. But he was more than that; he was a synagogue attendee, devout, God-fearing. Known for his generosity to the poor, always praying, always searching for something more. And yet, for all his good deeds and his rank, there was still an emptiness in his heart, an unfulfilled longing."

Paul continued, "One afternoon Cornelius is praying, just like any other day, but this time—this time, an angel appears. Not some dreamy, vague vision, but an angel as real as you and me."

Tertius looked up, clearly hooked. "An angel appeared to a Gentile?"

Paul chuckled, shaking his head. "Oh, that's nothing. Wait till you hear the rest." His eyes glinted with anticipation.

"Not only does an angel appear, but he tells Cornelius—this Gentile, this outsider—that God has been watching. That his prayers and gifts to the poor haven't gone unnoticed. And then he's given an assignment: send men to Joppa, bring back a man named Peter. Meanwhile, as Cornelius' men are making their way south along the coast—nearly thirty miles to Joppa—Peter is already there, staying at the home of a man named Simon, a tanner whose house sits right by the sea.

"You can imagine what that place smelled like—freshly treated leather, animal hides, and whatever else he was working on, all the time. Not to mention the customers coming and going. Probably a little chaotic. So Peter slips away, climbing up to the flat rooftop—a good place to be alone, to think, to pray…to get some fresh air. It's midday. The sun is high, the sea breeze rolling in, the city humming below. Peter's stomach starts growling. He's hungry. Probably thinking about food. But suddenly everything shifts. The sounds of the city fade, the rooftop vanishes—and he falls into a trance."

Tertius' mouth dropped open. Yes, Paul had the best stories.

Paul's voice lowered, drawing him in. "And then he sees it. A sheet—massive, like a sail—descending from the sky. It's twisting, shifting, alive with movement. At first maybe he thinks it's some kind of sign, some heavenly gift." Paul smirked. "And remember—he's starving. So for a split second maybe he's thinking, 'Is this food from heaven? Is this manna?'"

Tertius grinned.

"But as the sheet comes closer, he realizes it's not what he expected. The sheet is filled with creatures. Strange ones. A writhing mass of webbed feet and forked tongues, shrouded wings beating against each other in the tangle. Every kind of animal a devout Jew wouldn't dream of touching, much less eating. Then, clear as day, he hears a voice: 'Get up, Peter. Kill and eat.'"

Tertius stopped in his tracks, shaking his head at the absurdity. "But Peter was devout. He'd never—"

"No, he wouldn't," Paul interrupted. "Peter is horrified. He says, 'No way, Lord! I've never eaten anything unclean.' But the voice comes again, firmer this time: 'What God has made clean, don't call unclean.' It happens three times, Tertius. Three times before the sheet vanishes."

Paul let the weight of it settle, then continued, his voice almost conspiratorial.

"Peter is left there, stunned, trying to make sense of it. And right then the Spirit whispers to him: 'Three men are looking for you. Go with them, no questions asked.' Peter goes downstairs, and guess who's waiting at the door?"

Tertius exhaled. "Don't tell me it's Cornelius' men."

Paul laughed out loud, amused by the astonishment in the scribe's eyes.

They reached a spot where the path was shaded by trees, the sunlight dappling the ground with patches of light and dark. Paul slowed his pace, the next part of the story heavy on his tongue.

"When Peter gets to Cornelius' place, he's not just walking into a house—he's stepping into another world. Cornelius has gathered this whole group of people—family, friends, everyone he cares about. They're all waiting, eyes wide, hearts open, ready to hear what Peter has to say."

Tertius shook his head as he imagined the scene. At that time, for a Jew to enter a Gentile's house wasn't just unusual—it was practically unthinkable.

"But Peter," Paul continued, "he's still turning that vision over in his mind, trying to make sense of it. And then as he's standing there in Cornelius' house, looking around at all these Gentiles gathered before him—it clicks. He tells them straight, 'You know, it's against our law for a Jew to associate with or visit Gentiles. But God has shown me that I should not call anyone impure or unclean.'"

Tertius' eyes widened. "So the vision—it wasn't about food."

Paul pointed at him. "Exactly! It was about people. God was showing Peter, 'Stop calling the Gentiles unclean. I am bringing them in.' And for the first time, Peter starts to wonder—maybe, just maybe, the gospel isn't just for the Jews. It's for everyone.

"So Peter starts preaching, telling them about Jesus—how He healed the sick, how He was crucified, how He rose from the dead. And just as he's speaking about the forgiveness of sins—*boom!* The Holy Spirit falls on them. Right in the middle of his sermon. They're all filled with the Spirit!"

Tertius leaned in, his curiosity pulling him closer.

"They start speaking in tongues, praising God—just like the 120 followers of Jesus did back at Pentecost."

Tertius covered his mouth with his hand, a flicker of recognition stirring. He'd heard whispers of what happened in Jerusalem years earlier, where Jews began speaking foreign languages they'd never learned. Could this be the same? Gentiles too? Maybe those old prophecies about God's Spirit weren't just for Israel.

Paul nodded as if he could see the thought forming in Tertius' mind. "Peter just stands there, jaw on the floor. This went against everything he'd been taught. But there was no denying it—God Himself was making a statement: 'The Gentiles are mine, just like you.'"

Paul spread his hands, as if picturing the moment. "So what does Peter do? He does the only thing he can. He baptizes them right then and there. No waiting. No hesitation. That was the moment everything changed."

Tertius gave a low whistle, shaking his head in amazement. "And the other apostles...they accepted this?"

Paul's expression grew serious. "Not at first. Let's head back. We've still got a lot of work to do."

Tertius nodded, and they turned back, the path ahead familiar now.

"When Peter got back to Jerusalem and told the others what had happened, it was chaos. They couldn't believe he'd gone into a Gentile's house, let alone baptized them. But Peter, he laid it all out—the vision, the Holy Spirit falling on them, everything. They couldn't argue with that. They realized God wasn't just the God of the Jews—He was opening the door to the Gentiles too."[3]

"So," Paul continued, as they neared the house, "the question of whether Gentiles could be saved was settled. Or at least it was for Peter and most of those who were there. But the circumcision group—you know, those strict Jews who insisted that Gentiles must follow the Law of Moses—they weren't so easily convinced. To them, salvation still required circumcision and adherence to Jewish customs. It was a question that was hotly debated for the next few years."

Tertius could sense the tension in Paul's voice as they approached the house. He knew this was where things would get complicated.

"It all came to a head recently when some teachers from Jerusalem showed up in Antioch, where I was living at the time. They started telling the new Gentile believers, 'Unless you are circumcised according to the custom of Moses, you cannot be saved.'[4] Can you imagine that? Trying to lay the whole weight of the law on these new Gentile believers?"

Paul cleared his throat. "Barnabas and I weren't going to let that slide. We had a heated debate with them—this was the heart of the gospel on the line. But it became clear that we needed to settle this once and for all. So the elders of the church in Antioch decided to send a delegation to Jerusalem to sort it out with the apostles and elders there—with Barnabas and me leading the charge."[5]

As they reached the house, Tertius cast a sidelong glance at Paul, catching the fire still burning in his eyes. "And what happened when you got there?"

Paul reached for the door handle, then paused, glancing over his shoulder with the faintest flicker of a wry smile. "You'll see."

CHAPTER 9

THE COUNCIL

(GALATIANS 2:5–10)

Paul followed Tertius in, closing the door softly behind them. The quiet of the room was a stark contrast to the lively countryside they had just left behind. Both men moved toward the table, instinctively returning to their places, drawn by the unfinished task that awaited them.

Paul settled into his chair with a sigh, his hand brushing over the table as if reacquainting himself with the setting.

"Now," he began, "where did we leave off before our break?"

Tertius backtracked through the parchment, eyes skimming the last lines he had written. "You said you went back to Jerusalem after fourteen years."

Paul nodded. "Yes. That's what I was just telling you about. I, along with Barnabas, Titus, and some other believers, was sent to Jerusalem by the church in Antioch to settle the debate—did Gentiles need to be circumcised to be saved? The main council was going to be a gathering of apostles, elders, and recognized leaders from the church in Jerusalem. But before that larger meeting, I met privately with a few key leaders." His voice dropped slightly, as if sharing a secret. "I needed to speak with them away from the noise and pressure of the broader council.[1]

"Peter was there; James, the Lord's brother; John; and a few others. These were the men entrusted with leading the church, those who had walked with Jesus before the resurrection. I had no doubt we were led by the same Spirit, but I needed to be sure we were standing together."

Tertius nodded, following along as he reviewed what he had written before their break. "But then you mentioned some spies sneaking in. Did that happen *at* the council?"

Paul exhaled sharply. "No. That happened in the private meeting *before* the council—they had no business being there. I don't even know how they found out about it. The whole thing reeked of deception. That's why I call them spies."

Tertius narrowed his eyes. "But who *were* they, sir?"

Paul settled back into his seat, the lines on his face deepening. "Well, Tertius, these are the very ones corrupting the gospel—the ones I'm confronting in this letter. Whether it's the same individuals or not doesn't matter. It's the same spirit. It didn't just pop up in Galatia out of nowhere. I've been dealing with it from the very start. Like weeds sown among the wheat—just as Jesus warned us about! These people are what I'd call 'false siblings.' They come across as believers, as part of our spiritual family, but they're not."[2]

Tertius was taken aback by the bluntness of Paul's words. "So you're saying these people aren't even true followers of Christ?"

Paul shook his head. "I know it's a serious accusation, but I don't make it lightly. These Judaizers might claim to follow Christ, but their actions speak volumes. They're not just misguided believers; whether they realize it or not, they're working for the enemy!

"Picture this." He leaned in, his voice tight. "We're in a private meeting, gathered in the home of one of the brothers. The conversation is rich, edifying. We're digging into the heart of the gospel—what it really means to be saved, what it really means to follow Christ. Then—a knock at the door."

Paul rapped his knuckles against the writing desk, the sharp sound cutting through the quiet room. Tertius flinched.

"One of the brothers gets up to answer," Paul continued. "The door swings open, and these guys walk in. I'd never seen them before, but the moment they stepped inside I knew something was off. They didn't say anything at first. Just stood there, looking around, eyes flicking from face to face, sizing us up. Then the questions started. The debates. But it wasn't real discussion—it was manipulation. A slow, deliberate push to back us into a corner, to force the apostles to side with them. And just when I thought they couldn't get any bolder, they went for the jugular. They'd seen Titus waiting outside—obviously a Gentile. Their voices sharpened. Their eyes locked onto me. They demanded to know: 'Has he been circumcised?'"

"What did you tell them?" Tertius asked, hanging on the story.

"I told them the truth—Titus had come to faith in Christ apart from the law, filled with the Holy Spirit just as we were. But that wasn't enough for them. They started pushing hard, demanding that Titus be circumcised right then and there."

Tertius shifted uncomfortably in his seat. "That took some nerve," he muttered.

Paul nodded, his expression darkening. "Yes. They saw him as a test case, a way to set a precedent. If they could get Titus, a living, breathing example of God's grace among the Gentiles, to submit to circumcision, it would send a clear message to all the Gentile converts: Faith in Christ alone isn't enough. They'd need to become Jews first and get circumcised to be truly accepted."[3]

Tertius was spellbound. The scene played out in his mind—the crowded room, the tension in the air, the hushed whispers as these intruders moved in, trying to seize control of the meeting.

"What did you do?" he asked quietly.

Paul leaned back, his eyes smoldering with the fire of remembered defiance. "I stood my ground. I didn't budge, not an inch. And the apostles didn't budge either. It was unanimous. We wouldn't give in to their demands—not for a moment. We told them in no uncertain terms that we would not be enslaved again by the law. Christ had set us free, and we were going to stay free."

Tertius leaned back with a long exhale, letting the weight of the story slip from his shoulders. Suddenly, his eyes widened.

"Wait a moment," he said, sitting up straighter. "We haven't even touched on the real reason you went to Jerusalem yet, have we?"

Paul shook his head. "No, the Jerusalem Council happened a couple of days later. This is where everything would be officially settled. The elders were there, the Twelve were there, and of course so were those of the circumcision group. It wasn't just discussion anymore. This was the moment when the church would either stand on the truth of the gospel or fracture under the weight of legalism."

"And the leaders? Where did they stand?"

Paul's faint smile carried a trace of relief. "We all stood together. It was a victory, Tertius. A win for the gospel. We held our ground, and the message of grace stood unshaken. But in truth, I already knew how it would go. The leaders had affirmed the gospel in private; we were on the same page before we ever stepped into the council. That final meeting wasn't about convincing them—it was about making it official, declaring before the whole church what had already been settled in our hearts. The discussion was long, the case was laid out, objections were raised—but in the end, the truth stood firm. The gospel of grace would not be burdened by the yoke of the law."

He paused for a moment, as if replaying the scene in his mind.

"It was a good day," he added quietly. "We returned to Antioch with a letter—one that stated the apostles' conclusion clearly and was sent to the Gentile churches as a message of encouragement and clarity. It basically said, 'We know some people have gone out from us and caused confusion, but they didn't have our permission. So we're sending Barnabas and Paul—men who've risked their lives for Jesus—to clear things up. It seemed good to the Holy Spirit and to us not to burden you with anything more than to avoid food sacrificed to idols, avoid blood and meat from strangled animals, and stay away from sexual immorality. That's it.'"

Tertius let out a breath, a smile creeping across his face. "Sounds like a happy ending."

Paul's eyes darkened. "Not exactly," he said, crossing his arms and looking away. "Those Judaizers didn't back down. Losing that battle only seemed to fuel their fire. They took their act on the road, trailing me wherever I went. Every time I preached and planted a new stronghold for the gospel, they showed up a few months later, pretending to be brothers, spreading their seeds of discord and false teaching. They know I can't be everywhere at once."

Suddenly, Paul's eyes blazed with renewed intensity. "That's precisely why we need to write this letter. It will be copied and spread far and wide, serving as a faithful witness in every church. It'll give them a solid foundation of gospel truth to stand on. They need to know I'm fighting for them. What happened in Jerusalem wasn't just for Titus; it was to protect the gospel for believers everywhere. In fact, let's write this, Tertius. Say, **'But we refused to give in to them for a single moment. We wanted to preserve the truth of the gospel message for you'"** (2:5).

Tertius wrote furiously as Paul continued.

"And the leaders of the church had nothing to add to what I was preaching. (By the way, their reputation as great leaders made no difference to me, for God has no favorites.)" (2:6).

Tertius looked up. "Their reputation means nothing to you? Then why go to Jerusalem at all?"

Paul's voice softened, but the fire still burned beneath it. "Don't misunderstand me—I respect them. But their status, their influence, their reputation—none of that gives the gospel its power. The truth stands on its own, not because important men approve of it, but because it is from God." He glanced at his scribe with a knowing smile. "But I'm getting ahead of myself. Write this:

"Instead, they saw that God had given me the responsibility of preaching the gospel to the Gentiles, just as he had

given Peter the responsibility of preaching to the Jews. For the same God who worked through Peter as the apostle to the Jews also worked through me as the apostle to the Gentiles. In fact, James, Peter, and John, who were known as pillars of the church, recognized the gift God had given me, and they accepted Barnabas and me as their co-workers. They encouraged us to keep preaching to the Gentiles, while they continued their work with the Jews. Their only suggestion was that we keep on helping the poor, which I have always been eager to do" (2:7–10).

Paul paused, waiting for Tertius to catch up, the sound of the reed pen scratching against the parchment echoing in the quiet room.

As Tertius reread what Paul had just dictated, a look of admiration crossed his face. "It's truly amazing, sir. All of you—Peter, James, John, you—working together like this, recognizing each other's gifts. It must have been incredible to see such great men of God coming together in unity."

Paul smiled, a knowing glint in his eyes. "It's easy to think that way, Tertius, but remember, we're all human. None of us is immune to disagreement or misunderstanding. In fact, you might be surprised at what happened next."

Tertius' curiosity was piqued. "What do you mean, sir? I thought everything was resolved in Jerusalem."

"In many ways, yes, things were settled. We agreed on the gospel and on our respective missions. But unity doesn't mean uniformity, and even among us there were moments of tension."

Tertius nodded in agreement. He could tell there was more to the story, but Paul wasn't ready to share it just yet.

"But they did recognize you and welcome you, right?" Tertius asserted, as if to remind Paul, despite whatever else might have transpired.

"Yes, they did." Paul softened. "They are my brothers. We have different gifts and callings from God, but I need them and, if I may say so, they need me too."

Tertius smiled, feeling the warmth of Paul's words as he continued. "Each of us has a role to play, and that's what makes the church so powerful. Picture it as a body with many parts, each one doing its own thing. Just as a hand can't do what a foot does, and an eye can't do what an ear does. But when we all do our part, when we recognize and respect the gifts God has given to each one, we can accomplish far more together than we ever could on our own."[4]

Tertius dipped his reed pen back into the ink, anticipating Paul's next wave of inspiration.

"But Tertius," Paul said, his voice lowered, "unity is not easy. And unity doesn't mean that we compromise on the essentials. Some things are worth fighting for."

A chill ran down Tertius' back. Paul's eyes were wide and his expression serious. Something big was coming.

CHAPTER 10

THE CONFRONTATION

(GALATIANS 2:11–18)

PAUL TURNED ABRUPTLY to the table under the window, his gaze scanning the pottery fragments he had poured out of the bag earlier. His movements were deliberate, purposeful, as if a memory had suddenly resurfaced and he knew precisely what he was searching for.

His eyes landed on a particular piece—round and flat, with a smooth, slightly concave bottom. Its rim was irregular and jagged, suggesting it had broken off something larger. It stood out among the rest, thicker and sturdier, perhaps the base of a tall jar or vase.

He picked it up with care, turning it over in his hand. The inner face bore his own handwriting—familiar, urgent words hastily scratched onto the surface in dark ink. They were his prompts—notes he had written beforehand to guide his dictation.

At the top, a statement stood out, bold and emphatic—the very heart of what he was about to dictate. Paul read it aloud: **"Faith, Not Law, Justifies."**

Tertius watched as Paul examined the fragment. "What does it mean, sir?"

Paul's gaze remained fixed on the shard. "Keep listening. It will become clear as we write this next section."

A tense stillness settled over the room. Tertius felt it before he heard it. Paul's expression hardened, his voice carrying an edge as he began to dictate.

"But when Peter came to Antioch, I had to oppose him to his face, for what he did was very wrong" (2:11).

Tertius, absorbed in writing, suddenly froze. He looked up, confusion etched across his face. "Wait...what happened? You had to oppose Peter? The apostle Peter?"

Paul's gaze locked onto Tertius, but he seemed to look right through him with no intention of stopping his flow. "Yes, Tertius. Keep writing...

"When he first arrived, he ate with the Gentile believers, who were not circumcised. But afterward, when some friends of James came, Peter wouldn't eat with the Gentiles anymore. He was afraid of criticism from these people who insisted on the necessity of circumcision. As a result, other Jewish believers followed Peter's hypocrisy, and even Barnabas was led astray by their hypocrisy" (2:12–13).

Tertius' reed pen raced across the parchment, the drama unfolding in his mind.

Paul continued.

"When I saw that they were not following the truth of the gospel message, I said to Peter in front of all the others, 'Since you, a Jew by birth, have discarded the Jewish laws and are living like a Gentile, why are you now trying to make these Gentiles follow the Jewish traditions? You and I are Jews by birth, not "sinners" like the Gentiles. Yet we know that a person is made right with God by faith in Jesus Christ, not by obeying the law. And we have believed in Christ Jesus, so that we might be made right with God because of our faith in Christ, not because we have obeyed the law'" (2:14–16).

Paul paused, his eyes gazing down at the shard in his hand. Its rough edges pressed against his fingers, a reminder of the tension he felt back then. The words "Faith, Not Law, Justifies" stared back at him, anchoring his thoughts.

With purpose, he placed the shard in the middle of the table under the window, then continued dictating, his voice carrying the authority of the conviction that had driven him to confront Peter so boldly.

"For no one will ever be made right with God by obeying the law. But suppose we seek to be made right with God through faith in Christ and then we are found guilty because we have abandoned the law. Would that mean Christ has led us into sin? Absolutely not! Rather, I am a sinner if I rebuild the old system of law I already tore down" (2:16–18).

As Tertius finished writing, his hand trembled from the intensity of Paul's words. He looked up, his voice a mixture of awe and disbelief. "I still can't believe you confronted Peter...publicly!"

Paul nodded, the memory still sharp. "In this case, it was necessary, Tertius. The truth of the gospel was at stake. Peter's actions threatened to undo everything we'd fought for. And Peter had negatively influenced the entire believing community in Antioch."

Paul sat down, dropping into the chair like a hefty sack. Just telling the story seemed therapeutic, like a burden lifting from his shoulders. Tertius stayed quiet, realizing his listening ear was most needed.

"Antioch...it was beautiful there, Tertius. The church was thriving. Jews and Gentiles together, as it was supposed to be. Peter came up from Jerusalem, and at first everything was great. He was right there with the Gentiles, eating with them, talking, laughing, sharing stories. You should've seen the way they looked at him—like they couldn't believe it. Here was Peter, the rock, sitting at their table. It was like a stamp of approval, a sign that they belonged."

Paul's face darkened as he continued. "But then word came that some big shots were on their way—heavy hitters from Jerusalem. They were friends of James, the Lord's brother. And you know, Tertius, that carries some weight. Even Peter was intimidated by them."

"But Peter is one of the twelve apostles," Tertius scoffed. "What does he have to be afraid of?"

Paul exhaled sharply. "You obviously don't understand where Peter comes from. Out here in the diaspora, Jews and Gentiles share space. Not always comfortably, but it happens. They bring their own food. They keep their distance. They make it work.

"But in Jerusalem, it's a different story. Step under a Gentile's roof, and you're an outcast. Sit where one sat, and you're defiled. Touch their plate—you might as well be one of them. That's Peter's world. That's the world those men from James live in. They felt like just being there was already a compromise.

"But sitting at the same table? Eating with Gentiles? That was crossing the line. And Peter…Peter got scared, Tertius. You could see it on his face."

Paul crossed his arms and looked away, anger obvious in his voice. "It all came to a head at this big community meal. We were all there, Jews and Gentiles, eating together, laughing, talking. It was wonderful. Suddenly, the door creaks open, and in walk those guys from James. The whole room went quiet. They didn't say a word, didn't need to. Their presence alone changed the vibe. They walked through the room like they owned the place, disdain for the Gentiles written all over their faces.

"They didn't sit with us, didn't even try to mingle. They headed straight for this high table at the front of the room, set apart from everyone else. It was laid out with special food, prepared according to the strictest Jewish laws—with special utensils and everything. The whole thing was a show, a way to say, 'We're better than you, purer than you.' The room had been full of warmth, laughter…but after that it felt different. More like a battlefield. Lines were drawn. Unity went out the window."

Paul's eyes narrowed. "Peter noticed. Of course, he did. His laughter died in his throat. His mouth tightened. He kept glancing over at the high table nervously. The Gentiles sitting with him—they noticed too. Their smiles started to fade, replaced by confusion, by hurt. Then one of the men from James, this tall, thin guy with a face like a hawk, rose from his seat. He strode over to Peter, leaned in, and whispered something just low enough that no one else could hear. Whatever it was, it hit like a hammer. Peter went stiff, the color draining from his face. The man straightened, gave him a long, deliberate look, then turned and walked back to his seat. For a moment, Peter hesitated, like he was weighing his options. But it didn't last long. He stood up and walked away from the Gentiles, just like that. The look on their faces, Tertius…it was like they'd been slapped. Peter, the rock, had just turned his back on them."

Paul uncrossed his arms as he leaned back, the anger still there but mixed with something else, something like disappointment.

"From that moment on, Peter kept his distance. He wouldn't sit with us anymore, wouldn't share a meal. It was like he'd gone back to the old Peter, the one who didn't understand what Christ's death really meant. He stuck close to the men from James, trying to blend in with them, pretending that he was above the Gentiles. Then other believers from among the Jews started to sit apart from us too. Even Barnabas!"

Tertius hesitated. "But isn't Barnabas one of your good friends?"

Paul dropped his head as a heavy silence filled the room. After a long moment, he exhaled—a slow, weary breath.

"We were like brothers. We had been through thick and thin together."

He fell quiet again, his gaze lowered, eyes unfocused. The memory was painful—personal in a way Tertius could not fully understand.

"I mean, Peter's behavior shocked me. I was truly disappointed in him. But Barnabas?" Paul shook his head. "That one really hurt. We fought side by side for the Gentiles in Antioch…and again in Jerusalem. He was a champion for the gospel. A man I would have trusted with my life. And then, just like that, he pulled away. Not just from the Gentiles—from me. One moment we were brothers in the fight. The next, I was standing there alone. Abandoned."

Paul rubbed a hand across his face. "If even Barnabas could be led astray, don't you see, Tertius? This isn't just a misunderstanding. This is something deeper, more dangerous. If he—of all people—could be deceived, what chance do the others have?"

He straightened, his voice steadier now, jaw set. "And that's why I couldn't let Peter's actions go unanswered. I couldn't stay silent. I wouldn't. I stood up, looked Peter dead in the eyes, and laid it out for everyone to hear. I said, 'You're not fooling me, Peter. I know how you live when no one is watching. You eat with Gentiles, laugh with them, share their food, live like them. You don't hold to these purity laws when it's just us. You and I both know the law doesn't justify anyone. So why now? Why are you trying to force the Gentiles to follow rules you don't even keep yourself?'

"It was a tense moment, as you can imagine. But I wasn't done. I said, 'Tell me, Peter—when did Christ's blood stop being enough? Wasn't it enough when the Holy Spirit fell at the house of Cornelius? Wasn't it enough when we broke bread together, when you knew—you knew—that God had made no distinction between Jew and Gentile? And now, because these men from James show up, you act like all of that never happened?'

"I made it plain. The gospel isn't about following the law. It's about faith in Jesus Christ, nothing else. That's the truth we live by. And I wasn't about to let anyone—including Peter—undermine it."

Tertius blew out his breath, his shoulders slumping as the story ended. "It's hard to believe Peter, of all people, could stumble like that."

Paul's gaze softened just a little. "Fear does strange things to people. Even Peter wasn't immune. But that's why we must stay vigilant. The truth of the gospel is too important to let fear or tradition twist it. Even if it means standing up to someone we admire."

CHAPTER 11

THE OLD WALL

(GALATIANS 2:17–18)

IT WAS MIDMORNING, and the day was already warm, the kind of heat that promised a sweltering afternoon. Outside, the world had come alive—voices calling across the fields, the bray of a donkey, the occasional creak of a wooden cart rolling over dry earth.

Inside the room, the air was still charged with the energy of Paul's story about his confrontation with Peter. Tertius, leaning over the parchment, read back what he'd just written, a puzzled look crossing his face.

"Sir, can I ask you something?"

Paul nodded. "Go ahead."

"You said, **'No one will ever be made right with God by obeying the law.'** I get that. But the next part—I want to make sure I've got it right. You said, **'But suppose we seek to be made right with God through faith in Christ and then we are found guilty because we have abandoned the law. Would that mean Christ led us into sin? Absolutely not! Rather, I am a sinner if I rebuild the old system of law I already tore down'**" (2:17–18).

Tertius glanced up, brow furrowed. "This part about tearing down and rebuilding—I don't get it. It makes it sound like the law was…I don't know, an old building or something."

Paul's eyes flickered with approval. "You're close. Think bigger.

Think of the temple wall—the one that divides Jew from Gentile. You know the rule. If a Gentile crosses that gate, he can be put to death."

Tertius stiffened. He could see it—the stark boundary drawn in stone, the warnings posted for all to read.

"But let me tell you something, Tertius. That wall in the temple wasn't just built with rock. It was built into us. In the mind of every Jew. Every Gentile. Everyone. It was a reflection of human nature itself—the instinct to divide, to classify, to elevate 'us' over 'them.' Culture. Status. Nationality. We build walls out of anything we can find.

"Jesus didn't just chip away at it. He destroyed it. Jew or Gentile, male or female, rich or poor—we're one body now. One family in Christ. To live in that freedom isn't sin, it's grace. But to rebuild that old wall after it's been torn down—*that* would be a sin. A great one!"

Paul's finger hit the table with a thud. "That's exactly what Peter was doing. The moment he backed away from the Gentiles, he started stacking the rubble, rebuilding that wall. Brick by brick. And if he had finished, he wouldn't just be cut off from them—he'd be cut off from Christ. Because I promise you, Tertius—Jesus wouldn't be on his side of the wall."

Tertius' eyes widened. "I think I see it now. If someone rebuilds that wall, it means they still believe they need the law to be justified. That would be like saying Christ's sacrifice wasn't enough. That wall wouldn't just divide people—it would cut them off from grace."

Paul gave a small nod. "Now you're catching on. To rebuild that wall would be to say that following Christ was a mistake. It's a denial of everything He did for us."

Tertius tightened his grip around the pen. "That helps a lot, sir. Thank you."

Paul's smile broadened. "Shall we continue?"

"Yes, sir. I'm ready," Tertius said, dipping his pen in the inkwell.

CHAPTER 12

HE DIED FOR ME

(GALATIANS 2:19–21)

PAUL'S VOICE CARRIED a steady rhythm as he dictated, each word deliberate, as if he were chiseling them into stone.

"For when I tried to keep the law, it condemned me. So I died to the law—I stopped trying to meet all its requirements—so that I might live for God. My old self has been crucified with Christ. It is no longer I who live, but Christ lives in me. So I live in this earthly body by trusting in the Son of God, who loved me and gave himself for me" (2:19–20).

Tertius' reed pen scratched hurriedly across the parchment, capturing Paul's words almost as quickly as they came. But then Paul's voice changed—a subtle shift that made Tertius glance up. His hand froze mid-stroke just in time to catch a tear welling up in Paul's eye, slipping free and tracing a solitary path down his cheek.

"Are you all right, sir?" Tertius asked, lowering his pen, his voice tinged with concern.

Paul wiped the tear away with the back of his hand. "Yes, I'm fine. More than fine. I'm...overwhelmed by the reality of it all."

Tertius sat back, lost in the moment. He was beginning to realize there was something very different, very special, about Paul. "I've never heard anyone speak of Jesus the way you do, sir. You speak as if you believe He's here, as if He knows you personally..."

Paul looked up, his eyes gleaming. "He *does* know me, Tertius. It's not just something I believe—it's something I know. Jesus loves me, and He died for me. It's not just a doctrine; it's the deepest reality of my life."[1]

A shiver ran down Tertius' spine. He had heard others speak of God's love and Christ's sacrifice, but never like this. Paul spoke as if describing a close friend, someone who had walked beside him through every trial, every joy, every sorrow.

Tertius watched Paul intently, sensing the raw intensity of his conviction yet struggling to fully grasp it.

Paul, noticing the uncertainty in his eyes, leaned forward, his tone softened but still insistent. "Think of Moses. Imagine if I told you that Moses loved you. How would you respond?"

"I...I would find it hard to believe, sir. Moses lived so long ago. He didn't know me. How could he love me?"

Paul's voice dropped to a near whisper. "But Jesus...He's different, isn't He? He's not just a figure from history. He's God! And He's alive! He sees you, Tertius. He knows your name. When He stretched out His arms on the cross, He wasn't just fulfilling a mission; He was loving you. This wasn't just for someone else or for the world in general—it was for you personally."

The room fell into a thick silence as the thought settled. When Paul spoke again, his voice was almost reverent.

"When I say that Jesus loves you, I mean it with all my heart. It's not just some empty phrase. You and I could say that we love everyone, but that's a figure of speech, isn't it? We don't know everyone—we can't love everyone. But Jesus, He's not bound by time or space. He's divine. I don't pretend to understand how, but somehow when He died on that cross, He didn't just die for all; He died specifically for *each*. He died for you, Tertius. Literally, consciously, intentionally—He loved you and gave Himself for you."

Tertius felt the magnitude of Paul's words. He stared down at the parchment before him, the pen forgotten in his hand as tears gathered in the corners of his eyes. The truth Paul was speaking was almost too good to be true, yet it was undeniably real. He had always thought of Christ's sacrifice as a grand gesture for humanity, but never had he considered it so intimately, so personally.

Paul gazed out the window. "My loyalty is to Christ, Tertius, not to Moses—not to the law. The law didn't love me. The law didn't die for me. But Jesus did! I won't turn my back on Him, and I won't insult His sacrifice by trying to improve on it. When Jesus cried out, 'It is finished,' the debt was paid in full, once and for all. There's no room for anything else—His grace is enough, His work is complete, and I won't try to add my own pathetic effort to it."

Tertius looked up, his spirit soaring from Paul's impassioned words.

"Sir, when you speak like this, I begin to understand why you're so adamant about correcting the Judaizers."

Paul rubbed his eyes, his voice softened by emotion. "What do you mean, Tertius?"

"I mean, when you describe the gospel, it's so personal, so beautiful, so powerful and deep. The law seems impotent by comparison, like the light of a lamp being overwhelmed by the sun."

Paul nodded, an approving smile forming on his face. "That's a good analogy. And even a billion years after the lamp burns out, the sun will still be blazing. That's God's love—it never fades. And for all eternity, the cross will never lose its power."

Tertius shook his head slowly, still trying to absorb it all. "It's so…vast."

"It is," Paul agreed. "And that's why we

can never go back, Tertius. To do so would be to treat the grace of God as meaningless. Write this, **'I do not treat the grace of God as meaningless. For if keeping the law could make us right with God, then there was no need for Christ to die'"** (2:21).

CHAPTER 13

CHILDREN OF FAITH

(GALATIANS 3:1–9)

Tertius looked at Paul, concern etched into his features. "Sir, you've preached this gospel to the Galatians, haven't you?"

"Of course I have, many times—through tears, with all the passion I have," Paul replied, frustration in his voice. "I've preached my heart out. I've painted the picture so clearly; it's like they've seen Christ crucified right there in front of them."[1]

"Then how could they go back?" Tertius asked. "My heart quakes just hearing you talk. How could anyone turn away from such truth?"

Paul closed his eyes. "Because they've been deceived, Tertius. The Judaizers came in with their smooth talk and their appeal to the flesh. They prey on human pride, on that urge to earn a place, to boast, 'I did this. I kept the law. I made myself righteous.'"

The tension in the room was palpable.

"It's a lie as old as Eden," Paul continued. "These Judaizers are snakes. Their eyes gleam with false promises, their tongues flicker with deceit. Just like the serpent tricked Eve in the garden, convincing her she could be like God by eating that forbidden fruit, these men lure people in, making them believe they can make themselves righteous through the works of the law."

Paul's voice grew fiercer, every word crackling with intensity.

"Do you know how a snake hunts, Tertius? It doesn't chase a bird. No, it locks eyes with it, mesmerizing it, holding it in a cold, steady gaze until the bird is frozen, unable to move, unable to escape. And then, when the bird is completely helpless, the snake strikes, swallowing it whole."

Tertius shuddered at the vivid imagery.

"That's what the Judaizers have done," Paul said. "They've fixed their gaze on these new believers, hypnotizing them with their false teachings until they're helpless, dragging them away from the freedom of Christ and back into the chains of the law."

Suddenly, his exasperation boiled over. Paul sprang to his feet, eyes blazing with a holy fury. "Oh, foolish Galatians!" he cried out, his voice echoing through the room. "Who has given you the evil eye?"

He paused, struggling to find the right words to capture the storm of emotions surging within him.

"Write, Tertius. Write it down now!" he commanded suddenly, realizing there was no better way to pour out the depths of his heart. **"Oh, foolish Galatians! Who has cast an evil spell on you? For the meaning of Jesus Christ's death was made as clear to you as if you had seen a picture of his death on the cross. Let me ask you this one question: Did you receive the Holy Spirit by obeying the law of Moses? Of course not! You received the Spirit because you believed the message you heard about Christ. How foolish can you be? After starting your new lives in the Spirit, why are you now trying to become perfect by your own human effort? Have you experienced so much for nothing? Surely it was not in vain, was it? I ask you again, does God give you the Holy Spirit and work miracles among you because you obey the law? Of course not! It is because you believe the message you heard about Christ"** (3:1–5).

Paul turned sharply toward Tertius, his eyes burning with intensity. "Did you get all of that?"

"I think so, sir," Tertius said, his pen a blur of motion.

Paul waited for his scribe to catch up, his next words already forming on his lips.

"Got it, sir," Tertius said. Paul was on a roll now. Without even a warning, he launched into his next dictation.

"In the same way, 'Abraham believed God, and God counted him as righteous because of his faith'" (3:6).[2]

Tertius finished writing. He put the pen down and snapped his wrist, as if trying to revive his right hand. Beads of sweat had formed on his forehead as the warm room and the intensity of his work became apparent.

"Are you OK?" Paul asked. "Do you need a break?"

"No, sir, I'm fine. We can continue."

"Good." Paul replied. "Now write, **'The real children of Abraham, then, are those who put their faith in God'**" (3:7).

Tertius hesitated. He glanced back at the last sentence he had scribbled in such haste that he hadn't even paused to consider its full meaning.

"Now what's the matter?" Paul asked, sensing his hesitation.

"Well, sir, I've been with you up to this point, but I'm struggling with this. I know it's not my place to challenge you, but perhaps, for my own peace of mind, you could help me understand?"

"Of course, Tertius," Paul replied with a steady gaze. "What's bothering you?"

Tertius chose his words carefully.

"Well, sir, you and I are Jews. We are the people of God. Abraham is our forefather. Our people have cherished this identity for thousands of years. We've been persecuted for it, disciplined by God because of it. We take immense pride in it; it's our heritage—something we treasure. But now I hear you saying that all that's required to be a child of Abraham is to put faith in God—which means anyone can be a child of Abraham. Doesn't that…cheapen the status?"

"There are two things you need to get," Paul said, planting

his foot on the chair and leaning forward, his eyes locking onto Tertius'. "First, the reason Abraham was counted as righteous in the first place was because he believed God. Remember what the Scriptures say? 'Abraham believed God, and it was counted to him as righteousness.'"

"Yes, sir. It says so in Genesis," Tertius said, sensing that Paul was about to elaborate.

"And what was the context of that, Tertius?" Paul asked, his tone inviting reflection, urging the young scribe to think deeper.

"Well, sir," Tertius began, gathering his thoughts, "God told Abraham that he would have offspring as innumerable as the stars. But Abraham and Sarah were too old to have children. In the natural, God's promise was impossible, but Abraham believed God anyway."

Paul smiled, a glimmer of approval in his eyes. "Yes. But let's pause for a moment, Tertius, and really step into that story." He softened his tone.

"Imagine the vast night sky over the empty lands of Canaan, where Abraham lived. Picture him, an old man, way past his prime, standing under the heavens. The stars above him, countless and shining, like diamonds scattered on a black velvet cloth. Each one a reminder of what seemed impossible—a future as bright and endless as those stars."

Paul let the image linger, giving Tertius a moment to fully take it in before he continued. "But think about the impossibility of that promise. Abraham wasn't just old; he was ancient.[3] And Sarah? She'd been barren her whole life. The years had long robbed them of the chance to have children. By all natural logic, there was no hope, no reason to believe that a child could ever come from their union."

He leaned in closer, his voice dropping to a whisper, as if sharing a secret long kept.

"And yet right in that moment of impossibility, God spoke: 'Look toward heaven, and count the stars, if you can. So shall your offspring be.' Can you feel it, Tertius? The tension in that silent night, the desperation of an impossible promise, an old man's heart caught between the harsh reality of his life and the call to believe?"

Tertius nodded slowly, his imagination painting the scene.

"Now," Paul continued, "Abraham could have doubted. He could have laughed off the promise, just as Sarah did. But he chose to believe. Not because it made sense or because there was proof, but because he trusted the One who made the promise. He looked at those stars and believed that the God who created them could do the impossible. It was that faith, Tertius—simple, unshakable trust—that was counted as righteousness. Not his deeds, not his heritage, not his strength, but his faith.

"But here's what's easy to miss. When Abraham believed God's promise—that through his offspring the world would be blessed—it wasn't just about Isaac. It was pointing forward to Someone far greater. The true seed of Abraham. The One through whom the blessing would come to every nation.

"And years later, when God asked Abraham to offer Isaac on Mount Moriah, the picture became even clearer: a beloved son, laid on the altar, a substitute offered, and a promise that 'on the mountain of the Lord it will be provided.' It was a shadow of something greater—something only God could fulfill."

Paul's voice grew gentler.

"Abraham didn't know the name of Jesus, but he trusted the God who made the promise—and the God who would fulfill it. That's what God saw. That's what He honored. In fact, in a sense, the gospel was preached to Abraham ahead of time."

Tertius squinted. "What do you mean?"

"God's promise—that all nations would be blessed through him—was good news that would require a Savior. Abraham may not have known the full picture, but he believed in the One behind the promise. Jesus said it Himself—'Abraham rejoiced to see My day, and he saw it and was glad.' That means Abraham's faith looked forward to Christ, just as ours looks back to Him. But it's the same promise. One gospel. One Savior. One kind of faith.

"So you see, faith is not our Savior—Jesus is. But faith is what takes hold of Him, both then and now."

Paul let the moment linger. Tertius was silent, the weight of it all settling in.

"If faith is what God valued in Abraham, making him the father of many nations, then wouldn't it be faith that makes us his true children? The promise wasn't just about physical descendants; it was always about a lineage of faith—a spiritual heritage. The faith that made him the father is the same faith that makes us the children. Does that make sense?"

"Yes, sir!" Tertius blurted, sitting up straighter in his chair.

"But there's more." Paul took his foot off the chair and began to pace. "Do you realize that the Scriptures themselves saw this coming? That people from all nations—including the Gentiles—would be declared righteous by God simply because of their faith?"

Tertius' mouth was slightly open as he searched his memory, trying to follow where Paul was leading.

Paul jumped in, answering his own question. "Remember, God told Abraham that every nation on earth would be blessed through him. What does 'through him' mean? Is it just through his physical descendants? No! It's through his faith. That's the key!"

He gestured for Tertius to write. "Put it like this: **'What's more, the Scriptures looked forward to this time when God would make the Gentiles right in his sight because of their faith. God proclaimed this good news to Abraham long ago when he said, "All nations will be blessed through you"'"** (3:8).[4]

Tertius' pen flew across the parchment. When he looked up, his eyes were blazing with understanding.

"Yes! I think I've got it...Abraham wasn't just the first to believe—he set the pattern for everyone who would come after him. That's why he's called the father of many nations. The true children of the promise aren't defined by ancestry but by faith—those who believe as he did. It's amazing!"

Paul's eyes gleamed with satisfaction. "Exactly, Tertius! The Judaizers want the Galatians to think that becoming Abraham's true heirs requires circumcision—that without the law, they're outsiders. But they've missed the whole point of the promise! Abraham was counted as righteous *before* the law, *before* circumcision—because of faith alone. And that's the pattern. It's not those who bear Abraham's blood but those who share his faith who inherit the promise. The Gentiles don't need to become Jews to belong—they already belong through faith.

"Let's bring it home now. Write, '**So all who put their faith in Christ share the same blessing Abraham received because of his faith**'" (3:9).

CHAPTER 14

BESIDE THE SEA

THE MIDDAY SUN hung high, pouring its relentless heat through the window. The small room felt stifling, the warmth mingling with the intensity of their discussion. Tertius wiped his forehead with the back of his hand, smearing sweat as he finished writing. His heart was still soaring from Paul's revelation, but the heat was quickly dragging his enthusiasm back to earth.

Paul, who had been pacing, finally noticed the exhaustion on Tertius' face. He paused mid-step, glancing toward the window. "It's like an oven in here, isn't it? I think we could both use a break. Let's grab something to eat and cool off a bit."

Tertius nodded eagerly, setting his reed pen aside with a sigh of relief. Paul gave the jug of water a little shake. "Needs a refill," he said, as he picked up the cups, one placed inside the other.

They stepped out into the courtyard and the shade of a sprawling fig tree—a welcome relief from the stuffy room. Making their way to the storage area, they gathered a modest meal: bread that was still soft, a handful of olives, a cluster of figs, and a small wedge of cheese.

Tertius grabbed a folded cloth from a nearby shelf, shaking it out to ensure it was clean before tucking it under his arm. Paul dipped the near-empty pitcher into a barrel filled with water, submerging it just enough so that water rushed in over the lip and filled it to the brim.

With provisions in hand, they left the house, following a path that wound up a nearby hill. Tertius fell into step beside Paul, the crunch of gravel underfoot mingling with the distant hum of cicadas. By the time they reached the top, Tertius was nearly gasping for air—but then he saw it. The view stretched wide before them, the Gulf of Corinth glinting in the sun like a vast expanse of silver-blue silk.

Tertius shook out the cloth and spread it over the slope, where tufts of wild thyme and dry grass clung to the hillside. Paul let out a low whistle. "Well, if that's not worth the climb," he said, lowering himself onto the cloth with a grunt and a smile.

Tertius followed, sinking down beside him. They looked out over the shimmering water, letting the gentle sea breeze cool their flushed faces.

"Sir," Tertius said, "I can't even express how grateful I am to be working on this letter with you. I know it's for the Galatians, but honestly, it feels like it's being written for me! Everything you've explained...it's like the pieces of a puzzle finally coming together. I see it so clearly now—Abraham's faith wasn't just a beginning; it was the pattern for all of us. To think that I, too, can be counted among the children of the promise, not by my heritage but by faith—it's amazing."

Paul leaned back, resting on his elbows as he gazed out at the sea. "I'm glad you see that, Tertius. It's the truth that sets us free."

He turned his gaze back to his scribe. "Is there anything else you're struggling to understand? Anything else weighing on your heart?"

Tertius looked out over the water, his mind sifting through the cascade of thoughts Paul's words had stirred up. "Oh, yes, sir," he admitted. "There is something that's been on my mind. A question came up earlier, but you were on a roll, and I didn't want to interrupt."

Paul raised his eyebrows in a gesture of invitation as he pressed a piece of bread and cheese together and took a bite.

Tertius spoke: "You asked the Galatians, **'Did you receive the Holy Spirit by obeying the law of Moses? Of course not! You received the Spirit because you believed the message you heard about Christ.'**"

Paul nodded, encouraging him to continue.

"Well, sir, I thought I understood the importance of receiving the Spirit," Tertius began, his gaze wandering toward the shimmering sea. "But when you told the story of Cornelius earlier, I felt there must be more to it than I realize."

He looked out toward the water, searching for the right words. "I mean, it's wonderful that Gentiles can receive the Spirit. I see that. But Israel was God's chosen people for thousands of years—marked out by the law, the covenant, the temple, the traditions. And then in one moment—just like that—Cornelius and his household received the Spirit and everything changed!"

He turned to Paul, eyes wide with curiosity and awe. "What was so significant about that occasion, sir? How could it shatter barriers that had stood for millennia?"

He pressed on. "And when you asked the Galatians whether they received the Spirit by obeying the law or by believing, it's like you used *receiving the Spirit* as proof—that the gospel is true, that everything has changed, that the way we relate to God is no longer through the law. That the old boundaries just…don't apply anymore. I suppose I just don't see why that—receiving the Spirit—is the thing that proves it."

Paul finished his lunch, washing it down with a gulp of water. He wiped his mouth and stared at Tertius, eyes narrowing as he weighed his next words.

"Tertius," Paul began, exasperation in his tone, "it's curious to me that someone as well-versed in the Scriptures as you would struggle with this. And haven't you heard what happened on the day of Pentecost, nearly twenty years ago?"

"Not really, sir," Tertius admitted, feeling heat creep up his neck. "I've heard rumors, snippets, but nothing official."

Paul shook his head, gazing toward the horizon. "Somebody really ought to write it down one of these days," he muttered, half to himself, half to the wind.[1]

Turning back to Tertius, his expression softened, and a wry smile formed on his lips. "Well then. Sounds like it's time for another story."

CHAPTER 15

RECEIVING THE SPIRIT

As he prepared to recount the story that had shaped the very foundation of their faith, Paul gazed at the Gulf of Corinth—a moment of calm before the storm he was about to describe.

"Let me take you back, Tertius," he began. "All the way back to the days of Moses. Do you remember when Moses stood before the Lord, weighed down by the burden of leading the people? God told him to gather seventy elders—men who could help carry that load. And then something incredible happened. The Spirit of God, the same Spirit that was on Moses, rested on those seventy men—and they prophesied. The power and presence of God flowed through them, just as it had through Moses."[1]

Tertius nodded as he listened, knowing the familiar story would take on new significance in Paul's retelling.

"But it didn't stop there, did it?" Paul continued. "When two men who hadn't gathered with the others also began to prophesy, Joshua urged Moses to stop them. And do you remember what Moses said?"

Tertius thought carefully and then answered. "I wish that all the Lord's people were prophets, and that the Lord would put His Spirit on them."[2]

"That wasn't just wishful thinking—it was a prophecy, pointing to something far greater. Moses longed for a day when the Spirit of God wouldn't be limited to a select few but would rest on all of God's people. But when would this happen? How could it happen? Moses himself told us."

Paul's gaze intensified as he continued. "Do you remember how God told the people through Moses, 'The LORD your God will raise up for you a prophet like me from among your brothers. You must listen to him'?[3] He was speaking of the coming Messiah, Tertius. Someone greater than Moses who would not only carry the full measure of the Spirit of God but would pour Him out on all who believe."

Tertius knew the prophecy well but had never seen it in this light.

"Now, think about the story of Elijah," Paul went on. "Right before the great prophet was taken to heaven in a whirlwind, Elisha asked for a double portion of his mentor's spirit. And you know the story—when Elijah was taken up into heaven, that same spirit that was on Elijah came upon Elisha. The Spirit of God passed from one prophet to another.[4]

"These were just glimpses of something greater to come. The prophets foretold it throughout our history. Like when Ezekiel spoke of a time in the future when God would give His people a new heart and put a new spirit within us.[5]

"And Isaiah," Paul continued, "spoke of the Spirit resting on the Messiah and of the time when the Spirit would be poured out from on high, changing everything. He talked about the Spirit bringing both conviction of sin and spiritual renewal.[6]

"But it was Joel who prophesied it most clearly: 'In the last days, I will pour out my Spirit on all people.'[7] This was always the promise, Tertius. The Spirit of God, not just for prophets, not just for kings, but for everyone."

Tertius nodded, the words of the prophets echoing in his mind. Paul pressed on. "This was the sign, Tertius. This is how we would know that the Messiah had come—not just with words or laws written on stone, but with the very breath of God entering the hearts of men."

Paul leaned forward, his eyes intense, as if willing Tertius to grasp the significance of what he was about to say.

"And then came John the Baptist, the voice crying out in the wilderness, calling people to repentance, preparing the way for the One who was to come. John baptized with water, but he spoke of another—One who would baptize with the Holy Spirit and fire.[8] That was the Messiah, the One we had been waiting for. And then…Jesus appeared."

Paul's voice softened as he spoke the name of Jesus, a mix of reverence and love.

"Jesus was the fulfillment of those ancient prophecies. Everything about His ministry pointed to the outpouring of the Spirit. He spoke of it often, especially as His death drew near. He told His disciples that He would send the Comforter, the Spirit who would guide them into all truth."[9]

Tertius closed his eyes. The pieces were falling into place—almost too fast to keep up. But Paul wasn't finished.

"Then came the crucifixion. The Messiah, the hope of Israel, nailed to a cross. The earth shook, the sky darkened—it felt like all hope was lost.[10] But in that moment of utter despair, the greatest victory was won. Three days later He rose from the dead, conquering sin and death once and for all. But Jesus' mission wasn't over yet. Before He ascended into heaven, He gathered His disciples and gave them one final command—to wait. 'Stay in Jerusalem,' He told them, 'until you are clothed with power from on high.' And then, as He was ascending, He reminded them of the promise: that they would receive power when the Holy Spirit came upon them. Like Elisha watching Elijah taken to heaven in a whirlwind, they watched Him go—and they waited for the mantle to fall."[11]

Paul stood and began pacing, energy surging through him as he spoke. "So they waited, Tertius. Can you imagine it? Staying in Jerusalem, gathered in that upper room, praying, anticipating, not fully understanding what was to come, but trusting that Jesus would keep His promise. Day after day, together, waiting. The tension must have been unbearable. And then, after ten days…"

Paul stopped, his hand slicing through the air as if to silence every sound. "And then it happened. Not a whisper, not a breeze, but a sudden, mighty roar. A wind like nothing they'd ever heard—as if the heavens were ripping open. The sound filled the whole house, shaking the walls, rattling the doors, sweeping through their souls.

"And it wasn't just the wind, Tertius—it was power. Raw, uncontainable power. They could feel it on their skin, in their chests, like the very breath of God had entered the room, wrapping around them, pressing into them."

Paul's voice grew stronger, eyes blazing. "That's when they saw it—fire. Not ordinary fire, not the kind that burns or consumes, but tongues of flame, bright and pure, descending from above. And then," he continued, his voice dropping to a rough whisper, "their mouths opened and words poured out—but not just words, languages. Languages they had never spoken before. The Spirit of God moved in them, just as He did with Moses and the seventy elders. But this time, they weren't only prophesying in Hebrew—they were speaking in the languages of the world!"

Tertius was on the edge of his seat, heart pounding as Paul painted the scene with raw intensity.

"The disciples couldn't stay inside. The Spirit wouldn't let them. The power surging within them drove them into the streets, up toward the temple,[12] their voices ringing out in a chorus of different languages. They must have looked like madmen—staggering, shouting, arms lifted, fire still burning in their eyes. It was morning, the hour of prayer, and the temple courts were already packed. The people had gathered for worship, unaware that heaven itself was about to interrupt their routine.

"And there, in the courts of the temple, the 120 stumbled in—still speaking in tongues, their faces alight with the fire of God. The crowd, interrupted by the strange sounds, stood in stunned silence. Each man and woman heard the wonders of God declared in their own native language."

Tertius' thoughts were racing. "I can't imagine what must have been going through the minds of the people gathered for prayer at the temple!"

Paul's eyes flashed. "They were utterly bewildered! It looked like a drunken mob. But then—Peter saw it. He understood. The veil lifted, and in an instant the entire history of God's promises aligned. Peter stood there looking at the chaos and knew—he knew for certain—this was it. This was the moment the prophets had spoken of.

"It was the fulfillment of what Moses longed for—and prophesied—when he said, 'I wish that all the Lord's people were prophets, and that the Lord would put His Spirit on them.'

"It was what Elijah's mantle passing to Elisha had foreshadowed.

"It was Ezekiel's dry bones coming to life.

"It was the Spirit poured out on all flesh, turning the wilderness into a fertile field, as Isaiah envisioned.

"And in that moment, Peter—the man who had once cowered before a servant girl, afraid to admit he knew Jesus—now stood before thousands, unshaken, emboldened by the Spirit burning inside him. He lifted his voice and declared, 'These men are not drunk, as you suppose. It's only nine in the morning! No, this is what was spoken of by the prophet Joel....'"

Paul exhaled sharply, his chest rising and falling.

"Peter preached the gospel, and three thousand believed that day. Three thousand![13] The temple courts became the birthplace of a new kind of people—neither Jew nor Gentile, but something altogether different. A people marked not by the law but by the Spirit."

Tertius sat in stunned silence. Paul could see the weight of it in his eyes.

He leaned in slightly, his voice almost fatherly now. "And that, Tertius, is why the Spirit's presence is so decisive. It's not an add-on. It's not an insignificant, subjective experience. It's the proof, the undeniable evidence, that God's promise has been fulfilled. And that's why I'm reminding the Galatians about their own experience of receiving the Spirit. Just like the 120 in the upper room—just like Cornelius and his household—they received the Spirit when they believed in Christ, not because they kept the law."

Paul straightened. "The Spirit's presence is the final word. The Spirit is the evidence that faith in Christ alone makes us God's people."

CHAPTER 16

IN HIM

WELL, TERTIUS," PAUL said, his voice light as he stretched his arms, "I think it's time we got back to work."

The scribe smiled and stood, bending down to gather the remains of their lunch. He carefully folded the cloth they had sat on, his gaze drifting toward the horizon, where the sun cast a soft sheen over the Gulf of Corinth. The sea rippled gently, stirred by the soft afternoon breeze.

Paul picked up the pitcher of water, handed the two cups to Tertius, and nodded toward the house in the distance. Without a word, they began walking back down the narrow path, the conversation still fresh between them.

Tertius, leading the way, glanced back at Paul as they descended. "Sir, can I ask a question in light of all you've said about the coming of the Spirit?"

"Of course," Paul replied, setting each foot carefully, the downward path more precarious than the climb.

"Well, the Spirit came upon people in the Scriptures too—on the prophets, priests, even kings—so how is it different now? What changed at Pentecost?"

Paul slowed his pace, his expression turning thoughtful. "That's a good question, Tertius. The Spirit of God was definitely active in the past. He came upon men like Moses, Elijah, even Saul when he prophesied. But what we're seeing now, since that outpouring at Pentecost, is different. It's...more complete and permanent."[1]

Tertius frowned slightly. "How so, sir?"

Paul stopped mid-stride. "Hold on," he said, lifting the pitcher of water. "Let me show you."

Tertius turned, watching as Paul reached for one of the cups and poured a steady stream until it brimmed. The surface caught the light, trembling slightly.

"In the past," Paul said, holding the cup aloft, "the Spirit came upon certain people—filling them, like this. Empowered for a moment. For a purpose. But it wasn't permanent."

He paused, then slowly poured the water back into the pitcher. The cup stood empty in his hand.

"Like this," he said softly. "Once the task was done, the Spirit would lift."

Tertius' eyes narrowed slightly as he focused. "But now?" he asked, his voice betraying his curiosity.

Paul smiled. He placed the empty cup back into the pitcher, submerging it completely, water rushing in from all sides as it sank to the bottom with a thud. "Now we aren't just filled for a moment. We are in the Spirit, and the Spirit is in us—like this cup, fully immersed. It's no longer a temporary filling. The Spirit doesn't just come upon us; He lives within us, and we in Him."[2]

Tertius' eyes widened as he stared at the pitcher. "So it's not just that we receive the Spirit, but that we are…part of Him? Like…one with Him?"

Paul nodded. "Correct. And one with each other as well, since we were all immersed in one Spirit—into one body. As a result, our very nature changes.

"Imagine taking a land-dwelling, air-breathing creature and placing it in the depths of the sea," Paul said. "But instead of drowning, it's transformed. It grows gills. Fins. It becomes something new—something that not only survives in that environment but can no longer live outside it. That's what happens when we are born of the Spirit. We're not the same anymore—we are entirely new creations. *In Him we live and move and have our being.*"[3]

They continued down the path, Paul's words lingering in the air like a tangible presence. "The Spirit in the past was just a glimpse, a foretaste. But now, through Christ, the Spirit has been poured out fully, not just on a few, but on all who believe. We are all immersed in Him, and He in us. We're immersed in God!"

As they reached the house, their conversation faded into a comfortable silence. But inside Tertius, something fresh was stirring to life. The Spirit of God, the very life of God—everything Paul had spoken was real. The Spirit wasn't just for prophets of old; He was here, now, with *them*.

CHAPTER 17

THE TREE

(GALATIANS 3:8–14)

TERTIUS AND PAUL stepped back into the house, their footsteps tapping softly against the stone floor. They set their lunch remnants on the bench against the wall at the entrance. Paul stretched his arms, a brief gesture to shake off the climb, and moved toward his familiar chair, positioned by the writing table across from Tertius. "Now then," he said, "where did we leave off?"

Tertius cleared his throat as he read aloud: **"What's more, the Scriptures looked forward to this time when God would make the Gentiles right in his sight because of their faith. God proclaimed this good news to Abraham long ago when he said, 'All nations will be blessed through you.' So all who put their faith in Christ share the same blessing Abraham received because of his faith"** (3:8–9).[1]

Paul nodded, his eyes lighting with remembrance. "Yes, that's right. Faith! Just as Abraham was made right with God because of his faith, so are all who put their trust in Christ. We've been building on that idea."

Paul leaned back, interlocking his fingers behind his head. His gaze drifted to the pottery fragments scattered across the table under the window. He stood and hovered over the shards, searching for something specific. Finally, he saw it—a curved shard with jagged edges where it had broken from the whole. He picked it up, eyes narrowing as he examined the words etched onto it. "Christ: Breaks the Curse," he read aloud, his voice filled with quiet conviction.

The words settled into the silence, refusing to vanish, as Paul glanced over the smaller notes scrawled across the fragment. He turned back to Tertius, eyes blazing. "We need to draw the contrast. We've talked about the faith and blessing of Abraham, but that blessing stands in stark contrast to something else—the curse of the law."

Tertius poised his reed pen above the parchment, ready. He saw the shift in Paul's posture—the sharpening of his eyes as he gathered his thoughts, preparing to dictate the next vital truth.

"But those who depend on the law to make them right with God are under his curse, for the Scriptures say, 'Cursed is everyone who does not observe and obey all the commands that are written in God's Book of the Law'"[2] (3:10).

Tertius froze mid-stroke. His pen hovered, a bead of ink trembling at the tip. He reread the words and set the pen down. Leaning back, he rubbed his temples, as if trying to shake the weight of the thought loose.

Paul watched him quietly for a moment, recognizing the internal struggle unfolding on Tertius' face. "Are you all right?" he asked.

Tertius sighed and shook his head. "Sir, I won't lie. This bothers me."

Paul dropped his gaze for a moment as a faint smile tugged at the corners of his lips—an unspoken recognition of emotions he himself had once felt. "I understand. Believe me, I do. Tell me, what's troubling you?"

Tertius ran a hand through his hair, searching for words. Finally, he met Paul's gaze. He tapped the parchment lightly with the butt of his pen. "This turns everything upside down, sir." His voice was quiet but firm.

He continued. "It's one thing to say that God makes the Gentiles right in His sight because of faith. After all, Abraham was declared righteous before the law was given. He didn't need to follow the law; his righteousness was based on his faith in God's promise. This makes perfect sense for the Gentiles. But then…to say that those who are following the law are under a curse—" He stopped, shaking his head again. "That's where it feels like you're going too far. You're telling me that law-abiding Jews are cursed because they can't perfectly keep the law? That's *huge*. It turns our entire system of belief upside down. This isn't just radical, sir. It feels…dangerous. It's the kind of message that gets a man stoned."

Paul gave a short, sharp breath and looked down, something unspoken flickering in his eyes. He placed his hands on the table and leaned in, a spark of defiance rising. "But it's true." His voice rang with quiet conviction. "And truth should never be silenced by fear."

Tertius looked away, uneasy. Paul was right about truth—but was this truth?

Paul's gaze softened, but his voice remained steady, edged with grit and determination. He could see it—the battle raging inside Tertius, the weight of old beliefs pulling against something new. Just a little more and the scales would tip.

"Tertius, I know this is hard. I can show you this in the Scriptures, clear as day." His tone softened. "But you'll have to let go of your preconceptions and trust the truth to lead you forward."

Tertius exhaled with quiet surrender. Paul's unwavering conviction was undeniable, and in that moment he remembered—Paul wasn't just speaking from knowledge; he was speaking from a deep, personal experience with Jesus. "Yes, sir. You're right. I want to learn."

Paul smiled. "Let's take this one step at a time. Tell me, do you remember where the passage I just quoted is found?"

Tertius paused, his gaze drifting upward in thought. "I believe it's near the end of Devarim,[3] when Moses was giving his final instructions to the people—just before he spoke of the blessings and curses, if I recall correctly."

Paul was pleased. "Very good. The words of Deuteronomy are clear—'Cursed is everyone who does not uphold all the commands written in the law.' And the people said 'Amen' to it, binding themselves to that covenant."

He leaned forward. "But here's the problem, Tertius—who, other than Jesus, has ever upheld all the commands?"

"No one."

Paul nodded again. "Which means everyone under the law is under its curse, right?"

Tertius sat quietly, turning over the logic. Paul's argument was airtight.

"Ezekiel said something similar, didn't he?" Paul continued. "'Anyone who faithfully obeys my decrees and regulations is just and will surely live.'[4] But let me tell you something—when my teacher Gamaliel came to that verse in Leviticus, I always sensed it troubled him."

Tertius frowned. "Why, sir?"

"Because he knew what every honest man knows—no one keeps the law perfectly. That verse has always been one of the more challenging parts of the Torah. It seems to offer life—but on a condition no one can fully meet."[5]

"So how do the teachers of the law account for that?"

Paul shook his head. "The best they've come up with is this—if you're committed to the law, if you keep the most distinguishing commandments, the ones that separate us from the Gentiles, then God will regard you as righteous. And at the top of that list? Circumcision."

Tertius straightened. "But that's not what the law says."

"Exactly," Paul said. "The real problem, Tertius, is that they cannot face the reality that no one can keep the law—that it condemns everyone under its authority. That's a grim truth to accept…unless there's a way out. And that is precisely where Jesus comes in."

Paul set the pottery shard back down on the table beneath the window. Reaching into the leather sack, he pulled out a small, corked container of resin. He unstopped it and dipped his finger into the sticky substance, applying the resin along the jagged edge of the first fragment—circular and thicker than the rest. Then, with equal precision, he picked up the next shard, the one inscribed with "**Christ: Breaks the Curse**." It was smaller, its edge revealing it had broken off from the first piece at a right angle. In that moment, the shape began to emerge. The first piece—the thick, rounded shard—formed the base of a vessel, a jar, waiting to be restored. Paul pressed the new shard firmly against the base, holding it steady as the resin set.

Tertius' gaze drifted to the remaining shards scattered across the table, each with words etched on its inner surface. At first he had assumed they were just ostraca,[6] scraps of pottery Paul had repurposed for note-taking, a common practice among scribes and scholars.

But now he saw it.

These weren't just random fragments. They had once belonged to a single vessel, one that Paul intended to rebuild, piece by piece.

This wasn't just an outline. It was a restoration project. And by the same token, Paul wasn't simply dictating a letter—he was building something, line upon line.

"Tertius, it's not just that the law can't save," Paul continued, "it's that anyone who tries to live by it is bound to be cursed by it. The law is perfect, but we're not. We can't keep every command flawlessly. And because of that, we fall short and the law condemns us."

Paul continued holding the shard in place, his back still to Tertius, waiting for the resin to set. "Write this," he said with conviction. **"So it is clear that no one can be made right with God by trying to keep the law"** (3:11).

He paused, giving Tertius time to capture the words before continuing.

"Faith—that's what gives life, not the law."

Tertius looked up briefly, his eyes bright with understanding. "Yes, sir! I'm getting it."

Paul, sensing the momentum building between them, smiled and pressed on. **"For the Scriptures say, 'It is through faith that a righteous person has life.' This way of faith is very different from the way of law, which says, 'It is through obeying the law that a person has life'"** (3:11–12).[7]

Paul had barely finished speaking when Tertius blurted out, "So *the way of the law* says a person will live by obeying it, but since no one can obey it perfectly, it can never give life. It only leads to a dead end—the curse you were talking about. But *the way of faith* says the righteous will live by faith. They're completely different paths! One is about striving, trying to earn righteousness through works. The other is about receiving it as a gift through faith. I see it now, sir!"

Paul turned to face Tertius, his eyes gleaming with encouragement. Without missing a beat, he continued: **"But Christ has rescued us from the curse pronounced by the law. When he was hung on the cross, he took upon himself the curse for our wrongdoing. For it is written in the Scriptures, 'Cursed is everyone who is hung on a tree'"** (3:13).[8]

Tertius stopped, his hand frozen mid-air as Paul's words sank in. "I've heard that verse so many times. We recited it in the synagogue. The elders quoted it from Deuteronomy: 'Cursed is everyone who hangs on a tree.'" His brow furrowed as he muttered the words to himself. "The cross…the tree…the curse. It's all there."

He sat back slowly, his heart pounding with awe.

Paul leaned forward. "Oh, but it's even better than that, Tertius. Jesus didn't just *remove* the curse of the law—He *replaced* it with a blessing! The very blessing God promised to Abraham, the one meant for all nations, has now come through Christ. We always thought the blessing of Abraham was something you had to be born into or work for. That's what we were told. That's what we believed. To receive it, you had to be born Jewish or convert—obey the law, follow the rules, bear the mark of circumcision.

"But the gospel changes everything. Christ has made the blessing of Abraham a gift, not a wage. A promise, not a prize. And it's for everyone—Jew and Gentile alike. Not because of pedigree. Not because of good behavior. The blessing of Abraham belongs to anyone who is in Christ—through faith."

Tertius blew out a slow breath. He leaned back, shoulders heavy, heart light.

Paul watched him, a knowing smile at his lips.

"Let's write it, Tertius," he said.

Without hesitation, Tertius dipped his pen into the ink, poised to capture Paul's life-changing words.

Paul began to dictate, voice clear and steady. **"Through Christ Jesus, God has blessed the Gentiles with the same blessing he promised to Abraham, so that we who are believers might receive the promised Holy Spirit through faith"** (3:14).

CHAPTER 18

THE PRIOR PROMISE

(GALATIANS 3:14–18)

TERTIUS LOOKED UP from the parchment, locking eyes with Paul.

"Sir, you just said, **'Through Christ Jesus, God has blessed the Gentiles with the same blessing he promised to Abraham, so that we who are believers might receive the promised Holy Spirit through faith'** (3:14). Are you saying that the outpouring of the Spirit is the fulfillment of the promise to Abraham? I've always understood that promise to be about land and descendants, something more…tangible."

Paul's gaze sharpened, his thoughts focusing on a question that touched the heart of a mystery revealed in the gospel. He considered carefully how to answer.

"Tertius," he said finally, "God promised Abraham that through his seed, all the nations of the earth would be blessed, right? What do you think that means?"

Tertius set the reed pen into the inkwell and sat back. His mind sifted through years of study, trying to recall anything he heard in the synagogue, searching for a precise answer.

"Well, sir, I've always understood it to mean that Abraham's descendants—the people of Israel—would inherit the promises, and as the chief nation in the world, we would teach the truth about our God to the nations."

"Yes!" Paul agreed. "But let's dig a little deeper."

Tertius leaned back in his chair, arms crossing instinctively as he waited for Paul to continue.

"In Hebrew," Paul said, "when God says, 'through your offspring[1] all nations on earth will be blessed,' is the word *offspring* singular or plural?"

"Singular," Tertius replied without hesitation.

"Right," Paul said, waiting for Tertius to connect the dots.

Tertius' brow furrowed as he considered what Paul's question truly meant. "But if it's singular, then it doesn't refer to all of Abraham's children." He glanced down at the parchment, rereading Paul's words as if seeing them for the first time. The thought felt strange—almost unsettling. If the promise wasn't about Abraham's descendants as a whole, then who was it about?

"One descendant," he murmured, more to himself than to Paul. His fingers drummed lightly on the table, his mind sifting through everything he'd been taught about the promise to Abraham. *Through your offspring all nations will be blessed."*

He looked up suddenly. "Could it be Isaac? I mean, he was the child of promise, right? The one God gave to Abraham in Sarah's old age?"[2]

Paul nodded slowly. "That's what many believe. And in a sense, Isaac was *a* fulfillment. But was he the *ultimate* fulfillment?"

Tertius frowned. "I suppose not. Isaac didn't exactly bring blessing to all the nations. The promise must go beyond him." He leaned back, running a hand through his hair. Then his breath caught. "It's the Messiah, isn't it? You're saying the promise to Abraham was always about Him?"

Paul smiled, his eyes gleaming.

"Yes, Tertius. That's exactly what I'm saying."

Tertius shook his head in amazement. "That makes perfect sense. We've always believed the Messiah would bring peace and justice—of course, the promise was always about Him. It was always about Jesus!"

But just as clarity began to settle, doubt flickered across his face again. He hesitated, still uncertain if Paul had truly answered his question.

"But, sir, what does this have to do with the Holy Spirit? You said that *God blessed the Gentiles with Abraham's blessing so that believers could receive the Holy Spirit through faith*. I'm trying to understand—how does Abraham's blessing connect to the Spirit?"

Paul leaned in slightly, his expression intent. "Let me ask you another question. How do we know Jesus is the Messiah? He's not physically reigning on earth, and peace and justice haven't yet filled the world. So how do we know, with certainty, that He is the One?"

Tertius stared at Paul, uncertain, the pieces still not quite fitting together. Where was Paul going with this?

"Remember when we spoke by the sea?" Paul asked. "We talked about Pentecost and how the Spirit being poured out wasn't just an event—it was the fulfillment of a promise. The promise that, in the last days, God would pour out His Spirit on all flesh."

Tertius closed his eyes, recalling the conversation. "Yes, sir, I remember."

"What did the prophets tell us about the coming of the Messiah, Tertius? What would be the sign of His arrival?" Paul continued without waiting for a response. "The outpouring of God's Spirit. That was the sign, the unmistakable evidence. Remember? The prophets foretold a new covenant, not written on stone, but on hearts—hearts transformed by the Spirit. That's what the Messiah would bring."

Paul turned toward the window, his gaze thoughtful. "Do you know how God revealed to John the Baptist that Jesus was the Messiah?"

Tertius frowned. "No, sir. I haven't heard that before."

Paul's eyes gleamed. "It's fascinating. God told John, 'The One you see the Holy Spirit descend on and stay with—that's the One who will baptize with the Holy Spirit.'"[3]

Tertius leaned in, sensing Paul was leading toward something profound.

"In other words, Tertius, John knew that when he found the One who baptizes with the Holy Spirit, he had found the Messiah—because the Messiah *is* the Baptizer!"

Paul faced Tertius, his eyes flashing with conviction. "Do you see it? God didn't have to directly tell John, 'Jesus is the Messiah.' Instead, He showed him through a clear sign. If Jesus is the One who baptizes with the Holy Spirit, then He is the Messiah. It's as simple as that! The outpouring of the Spirit was the proof—the sign—that Jesus is the One God promised to send. It was the defining mark of His mission."

Tertius' face brightened with clarity, but a question still lingered.

"But…there's more to it, isn't there, sir? Jesus, the Messiah, is still going to rule the nations and bring peace and justice to the world, right?"

Paul nodded. "Of course He will, Tertius. That's the future promise we hold on to. But here's the key: The outpouring of the Holy Spirit is the sign that the process has already begun. It's like God has made the first installment, a down payment on His promise."[4]

Paul's eyes gleamed as he leaned in, his voice rich with certainty. "And you can be sure of this—when God makes a deposit, the rest is guaranteed to follow." He paused and smiled, a sure sign that he was about to bring all the pieces together now. "So you see, when the Gentiles receive the Holy Spirit by faith in Jesus, they receive the down payment of the same promise made to Abraham. That's not only how we know they have been accepted into the family of faith, it's how we can be sure they will receive everything else promised."

Tertius shook his head in wonder. "It's astonishing, sir. I never realized how vast and profound the gospel truly is. And what you said earlier about the promise to Abraham being made to one descendant—it sets the stage for Jesus in a way I never fully understood."

"Yes, it's a critical point," Paul said. "It also helps us see why the promise to Abraham, fulfilled in Christ, goes beyond the law."

"How so, sir?" Tertius readied his reed pen as if anticipating Paul's next dictation.

"Well, imagine you sign a contract with someone. Once it's signed, you can't just ignore it or decide to change it whenever you feel like it, can you? Of course not! It's permanent, binding. And it's the same here. God made a promise to Abraham, to be fulfilled in his Offspring—singular—in Jesus. And He made that promise hundreds of years before the law was given to Moses."

Paul leaned forward. "Now tell me—can the law, which came 430 years later, cancel or change the promise God made to Abraham? Do you think God would just change His mind out of nowhere, break His promise and decide that now there's a new way to the inheritance?"

"No, sir. That would make God a liar."

Paul's voice lifted. "Write this: **'Dear brothers and sisters, here's an example from everyday life. Just as no one can set aside or amend an irrevocable agreement, so it is in this case. God gave the promises to Abraham and his child. And notice that the Scripture doesn't say "to his children," as if it meant many descendants. Rather, it says "to his child"—and that, of course, means Christ'"** (3:15–16).[5]

Tertius wrote quickly, following Paul's dictation.

"Do you see it, Tertius? If righteousness came through the law, then God's promise to Abraham meant nothing. But God doesn't break His word. He made the promise before the law was ever given—and He kept it in Christ."

"Yes, sir! Thank you for taking the time to explain this. It all makes sense to me now."

Paul met Tertius' gaze. "Now let's make sure the Galatians see it just as clearly. Write this: **'This is what I am trying to say: The agreement God made with Abraham could not be canceled 430 years later when God gave the law to Moses. God would be breaking his promise. For if the inheritance could be received by keeping the law, then it would not be the result of accepting God's promise. But God graciously gave it to Abraham as a promise'"** (3:17–18).

CHAPTER 19

THE LAW VERSUS THE PROMISE

(GALATIANS 3:19–22)

PAUL ROLLED HIS shoulders before settling back into his chair. The afternoon light streamed through the narrow window, casting soft shadows across the room.

Tertius shaved the tip of his reed pen with a small knife, fine curls of fiber falling to the table. As the shavings peeled away, his next question formed in his mind.

"May I ask another question, sir?"

Paul's eyes brightened. "Of course. What is it?"

Tertius ran the blade along the reed again, his focus split between the task and his thoughts.

"You've made it clear that the promise came first—long before the law—and that righteousness comes by faith, not by keeping the law." He paused, examining the sharpened tip. "So then…why did God give the law in the first place? What was its purpose?"

"That's a great question," Paul said. "In fact, why don't we answer that question for the Galatians as well. Write it like this: **'Why, then, was the law given? It was given alongside the promise to show people their sins. But the law was designed to last only until the coming of the child who was promised. God gave his law through angels to Moses, who was the mediator between God and the people'"** (3:19).

Paul rested his hands on the table. "The law was never meant to replace the promise, Tertius. That was never God's original intent—it was added because of sin. If sin had never entered the world, there would have been no need for the law. But sin has no place in God's ultimate plan for humanity, and neither does the law. Once sin is dealt with, the law has served its purpose."

Tertius considered this, but a shadow of confusion lingered on his face. "So the law was always meant to be temporary?"

"That's it! The law was like a *paidagōgos*—a guardian, like the tutors wealthy Greek families hire. It kept us on the path, but it was never the destination. Think about it—how disappointing would it be if God's ultimate plan was just a set of rules? No, Tertius—God had something *far* better in mind. *Jesus.* Once the promise was fulfilled in Him, the law's role as a path to righteousness ended. The promise is eternal; the law was only for a time."

Paul continued to dictate. **"Now a mediator is helpful if more than one party must reach an agreement, but God, who is one, did not use a mediator..."** (3:20).

Tertius frowned slightly. "Wait. You just said the law had no mediator. But Moses was the mediator, wasn't he? Moses stood between God and the people." His tone carried the confidence of someone pointing out an inconsistency.[1]

Paul nodded, his expression patient. "Yes, Moses was the mediator when the law was given, but I wasn't finished." He gestured toward the parchment. "I'm talking about something else now—the promise God made to Abraham. Let's make that clear for the Galatians too. Say it like this, **'But God, who is one, did not use a mediator when he gave his promise to Abraham'**" (3:20).

Paul lifted both hands in front of him, palms open as if holding two invisible objects in the air. "You have to see this, Tertius. I'm drawing a distinction—between the law on one hand and the promise on the other."

His gaze flicked between his hands, the distinction emphasized as much by his movements as his words. "When God gave the promise to Abraham, there was no mediator. It wasn't a two-sided agreement—it was a direct, unconditional promise from God Himself."

Tertius nodded but still looked puzzled. Paul noticed his hesitation and studied him for a moment.

"Tertius," he said softly, "I know you know this story well. But I want you to try something. Close your eyes."

Tertius looked at him, curious, then followed the instruction, closing his eyes.

"Now," Paul began, his voice dropping into a storyteller's rhythm, "picture the night when God cuts His covenant with Abraham.[2] God tells him to bring animals, cut them in two, and lay the pieces opposite each other with a path down the middle. Imagine that grisly scene. A heifer, a goat, a ram—hacked apart, their halves facing each other in the twilight.

"Blood pools in the dirt, dark and glistening. The air is thick with a metallic smell—the unmistakable stench of death. Abraham stands motionless. A nearby campfire crackles, shadows dancing across the severed remains. The path between the carcasses stretches before him like a bloody corridor. The night grows long, heavy with silence. But still, nothing happens. God told him to prepare the sacrifice, but He hasn't said when He will come. So Abraham just keeps waiting."

Paul paused, letting the imagery sink in.

"As darkness descends, a deep stillness envelops him. His eyelids grow heavy with the pull of sleep. Then suddenly, an overwhelming dread washes over him, sending tremors through every part of his body. The hairs on his arms stand up, as if sensing an unseen danger. The atmosphere shifts; an unnerving hum permeates the air, vibrating through the silence. Abraham is trapped in that space between wakefulness and sleep, unable to rouse himself.

"The hum grows louder, reverberating through his bones, making the stillness seem alive. It feels as if he's being sucked into another reality, the world around him warping and distorting. His limbs are heavy, his mind sluggish. All he can do is surrender to the pull. A deep, unshakable sense of foreboding tightens like a vise around his chest as he slips into a haze of surreal images.

"Suddenly, a smoking firepot and a blazing torch appear, floating in midair as though held by an unseen hand. They drift forward, slow and deliberate, illuminating the split carcasses as they glide between them. The ground trembles as these fiery symbols of God's presence pass through the bloody path.

"Then comes a sound. A voice. God is speaking—binding Himself to His promise with an unbreakable oath. Abraham tries to move, but he can't. All he can do is watch, helpless, as God seals the covenant alone, swearing by His own name."

Paul fell silent, his gaze fixed on Tertius. The room became still, the story fresh and vivid in their minds.

"Now, Tertius," Paul said, "when a covenant is made, both parties walk between the butchered pieces, right?"

Tertius nodded.

"Why do they do that?"

"It's a pledge—a way of saying, 'If I break this covenant, let what happened to these animals happen to me.' It binds both parties to the agreement, sealing it in blood."

Paul's eyes gleamed. "Exactly. But with Abraham there's a twist, isn't there?"

Tertius frowned, his mind tracing the familiar story—then his eyes widened as he saw it. "God made the promise *by Himself*," he murmured.

Paul smiled. "That's right. God didn't allow Abraham to walk through the pieces. God made the covenant alone, taking responsibility for both sides!"[3]

"So if the covenant is broken...the punishment falls on God Himself?"

"Yes. That's what makes it so extraordinary. God was promising to uphold the covenant, even if it meant bearing the punishment for our failure Himself. And that, Tertius, points us directly to the cross. When we failed to keep the covenant, God—through Christ—took the responsibility for our failure. It's Christ that makes us righteous, not the law."

After a moment of reflection, Tertius broke the stillness. "So the law did serve a purpose, but that purpose was never to make us righteous?"

"Exactly. The law served many purposes, but making us righteous was never one of them. The law restrained sin by imposing penalties, but now the Holy Spirit does that work within us. It set Israel apart from the nations, but now, through Christ, God is uniting Jew and Gentile into one family of faith.

"The law revealed God's character, but Jesus is an even clearer revelation. Most importantly, it magnified our sin—not just that we sin, but that even when we know what's right, we still do the opposite. Without the law, how would we see how far we've fallen? How would we even know the boundaries?

"But here's the problem. While the law exposes our sin, it can't cleanse us of it. It's like a mirror—you can see that your face is dirty, but no matter how hard you rub the mirror, it won't make you clean. The law leaves us trapped in the knowledge of our failure without offering a way out. That's why it could never bring life. It was never meant to *save*—only to show us our need for a Savior."

Paul's expression sharpened with renewed focus. "Write this, **'Is there a conflict, then, between God's law and God's promises? Absolutely not! If the law could give us new life, we could be made right with God by obeying it. But the Scriptures declare that we are all prisoners of sin, so we receive God's promise of freedom only by believing in Jesus Christ'**" (3:21–22).

CHAPTER 20

THE TUTOR

(GALATIANS 3:23–4:1–7)

PAUL STOOD, SLIDING his chair away from the writing desk and turning it toward the table beneath the window. Settling into the seat, he let his eyes scan the pottery fragments scattered before him. The vessel was slowly taking shape. His hand hovered over the jagged shards for a moment before selecting one. Its edges were rough, but the curve suggested it would fit perfectly with the others. He read aloud the words etched on its surface: **"The Law: Guardian, Not Savior."**

"That reminds me, sir," Tertius said. "You mentioned the law as a *paidagōgos*—a guardian. I know they tutor young boys, but I'm not entirely familiar with the concept. What exactly is the analogy you're drawing?"

Paul smiled, sensing the need for clarity. "Ah, yes. If you didn't grow up around wealth, you may not have had much interaction with families who use a paidagōgos. But remember, we're writing to Gentiles, and this is a metaphor they'll easily relate to. Let me explain it more fully so you'll understand."

As Paul spoke, he turned the shard over in his hand, carefully applying a thin line of resin along its edge. His focus remained on the pottery as he continued.

"In the Greek and Roman world, a paidagōgos is common,

especially in wealthy families. Picture a young boy, heir to a vast estate, destined to command servants and manage the household. But as a child, he's far from ready for that role."

Tertius watched Paul's hands press the shard into place, but his mind was fully engaged with what he was hearing.

"The boy is placed under the care of a paidagōgos—a trusted servant who oversees him every step of the way. At dawn, the tutor is there, waking him, guiding him through the day, teaching him how to live, how to speak, how to carry himself with the dignity his future position requires. He escorts him to school, shielding him from harm and bad influences. But the paidagōgos is not a parent—only a guide. He comes later, after the parents and teachers have already shaped the child's foundation. His role is secondary. And temporary."

Paul pressed the shard firmly into place. "That's the law, Tertius. A protector and guide—necessary but temporary."[1]

Paul glanced over at Tertius to ensure he was keeping up before continuing.

"The boy is no different from a servant while under the paidagōgos," Paul explained. "His every action is watched, corrected, and directed, under orders, until he comes of age. But once the child reaches maturity, the tutor's role is done. The boy is no longer under supervision—he steps into his inheritance. This is precisely how the law functioned. The law guided us, disciplined us, kept us from straying, but it wasn't meant to last forever. Now that the way of faith has come—now that Christ has come—we've reached maturity. We're no longer under the guardianship of the law."

Tertius nodded, his pen ready.

"Write this," Paul said. **"Before the way of faith in Christ was available to us, we were placed under guard by the law. We were kept in protective custody, so to speak, until the way of faith was revealed. Let me put it another way. The law was our guardian until Christ came; it protected us until we could be made right**

with God through faith. And now that the way of faith has come, we no longer need the law as our guardian" (3:23–25).

Tertius wrote swiftly, the words flowing onto the parchment. "Guarding and confining us," he murmured, thinking out loud.

"Yes, guarding and confining," Paul echoed. "The law was like a fence—it showed us where the boundaries were and helped to keep us from wandering off into deeper destruction.[2] That was a valuable and important service."

Tertius shifted in his seat, rubbing the back of his neck. "I understand what you're saying, but…it sounds suffocating. Like a child kept under lock and key, never free to step beyond the threshold."

Paul chuckled, shaking his head slightly. "That's the other side of it," he said, pushing himself to his feet, as if energized by the thought. "Protective custody places limits on a person's freedom—severe limits at times. That's why we need to be liberated from it to live a life of true freedom."[3]

Tertius nodded. "Because…we've come of age now, so to speak?"

"Yes." Paul's face softened into a smile. "We've come into maturity—through faith in Christ. And with that faith comes something far greater than what the law could ever give." His voice dropped to a reverent whisper. "Through faith in Christ, we've become sons and daughters of God."

Tertius' reed pen was poised again, ready.

"Write this," Paul said. **"For you are all children of God through faith in Christ Jesus. And all who have been united with Christ in baptism have put on Christ, like putting on new clothes. There is no longer Jew or Gentile, slave or free, male and female. For you are all one in Christ Jesus. And now that you belong to Christ, you are the true children of Abraham. You are his heirs, and God's promise to Abraham belongs to you"** (3:26–29).[4]

As Tertius reached the final line, he placed the pen back into the inkwell and flexed his tired fingers. The quiet of the room was broken only by the faint breeze outside. A question formed slowly in his mind as he massaged his hand.

"Sir, I understand that the law was like a guide, leading us to Christ and teaching us right from wrong. But now that we're in Christ and no longer under the law, I'm struggling to understand something. Without the law to define what's sinful and keep us in check, what stops us from falling back into sin? How does faith alone change us in a way that makes the law unnecessary? How does it ensure we live obediently?"

Paul smiled, recognizing the perfect moment to take the conversation to the next level. "That's a great question, Tertius, and it's precisely where we need to go next."

He gestured for Tertius to write, his voice steady as he dictated.

"Think of it this way. If a father dies and leaves an inheritance for his young children, those children are not much better off than slaves until they grow up, even though they actually own everything their father had. They have to obey their guardians until they reach whatever age their father set. And that's the way it was with us before Christ came. We were like children; we were slaves to the basic spiritual principles[5] of this world. But when the right time came, God sent his Son, born of a woman, subject to the law. God sent him to buy freedom for us who were slaves to the law, so that he could adopt us as his very own children" (4:1–5).

Paul continued, slowing his cadence to put emphasis on the next words.

"And because we are his children, God has sent the Spirit of his Son into our hearts, prompting us to call out, 'Abba, Father.' Now you are no longer a slave but God's own child. And since you are his child, God has made you his heir" (4:6–7).

Tertius finished writing and laid down his reed pen, deep in thought. "So Jesus buys our freedom—which allows the Father to adopt us as His children—which allows the Holy Spirit to live in our hearts."

Paul nodded slowly, encouraging Tertius to continue.

"So it's the Spirit within us that empowers us to do what is right?" Tertius asked, looking up at Paul for confirmation.

"Exactly. The Spirit accomplishes what the law could only demand—giving us the power to live as God intended. His presence in us is the undeniable proof of our adoption, the seal of our inheritance. So when a Gentile accepts circumcision, they're trying to earn a status that is already theirs!"

CHAPTER 21

SLAVES TO THE WORLD

(GALATIANS 4:8–14)

Paul leaned back in his chair, his hand absently tracing the edge of the table under the window as his thoughts drifted from the theological to something more personal.

Tertius, sensing the subtle shift in the atmosphere, set down his reed pen and waited.

After a moment, Paul spoke. "Tertius, persuasion is an art. It isn't just about presenting the truth—it's about making the truth convincing. There are three ways to persuade: *logos, pathos,* and *ethos.*

"Logos—reasoned persuasion, the use of evidence and structured argument; pathos—emotion, the deep feeling that moves a person to act; and ethos—trust, the credibility of the one speaking. So far I've built the case with logos. I've shown them why the law was temporary and why faith in Christ sets them free. Step by step, I've reasoned with them.

"But reason alone won't hold them. They need to *feel* the weight of what they're doing. That's the pathos part. This isn't just an error—it's a betrayal of what they know. A denial of what they've experienced. They're putting themselves back in chains, and I need them to sense that."

Paul's voice softened. "Then there's ethos. They know me.

They've seen my life. They've trusted me as their spiritual father. That's why I need to remind them of our history, of the love we've shared. This isn't just about proving a point—it's about restoring trust."

Paul's eyes met Tertius', a quiet understanding passing between them. "Now we bring it all together—truth, emotion, and trust—to show them what's truly at stake."

Tertius nodded with renewed focus, ready to capture the next words.

"Before you Gentiles knew God, you were slaves to so-called gods that do not even exist. So now that you know God—or should I say, now that God knows you—why do you want to go back again and become slaves once more to the weak and miserable forces of this world?" (4:8–9).[1]

Tertius wrote quickly as Paul's words tumbled out. He looked up with a crease of concentration forming on his forehead.

"Sir, are you comparing the law to idols? Surely, the law came from God, but idols…they represent demons."

Paul stopped pacing and turned back to the table, resting his hands on its edge.

"A good question, Tertius. No, the law itself isn't an idol. It came from God, and it served its purpose. But listen carefully—when people use it as a means to justify themselves before God, they are falling back into the same kind of bondage they once had under idols."

Tertius frowned, considering Paul's words.

Paul pressed on. "Think about it, Tertius. What were the gods of the Gentiles? The sun, the moon, fire, water—natural forces turned into objects of worship. But these idols had no life, no voice, no power. They depended on their worshippers to make offerings to them, carve their faces from stone, and move them. And still people gave their lives to them."

Paul's expression darkened. "But do you know what enslaved people more than the idols themselves? The system built around them. The rituals. The endless sacrifices. The desperate striving for favor that never came. And behind it all? Not just ignorance. Not just human folly. Something darker."

Tertius swallowed. "Spiritual forces?"

Paul nodded. "Yes. Forces that love to see people bound in systems that can't save them. Anything other than Christ—whether law or idols—is just another form of slavery. But now, Tertius, they know a God who knows them back. Not a distant force. Not a silent idol. The living God. The God who chose them. The God who calls them His own."

He spread his arms wide. "To be known by God—to be chosen by Him—is the greatest privilege under heaven. And yet they would trade it away? Return to feasts and festivals that can never satisfy? To a system that demands but never fulfills? They must not turn back, Tertius. They must press forward in Christ."

Paul pushed back from the table beneath the window and rose to his feet. With a firm grip, he turned the chair toward the writing desk and settled into it once more, now facing Tertius.

"Now comes the hard part."

Tertius glanced up. Paul met his eyes. "It's time to speak to their hearts." He tapped the writing table lightly, as if gathering his thoughts. "This is where ethos and pathos come in. They need to *feel* what they're doing. They need to remember who I am to them." He gave a half-smile. "Let's see if I can hold it together."

He gestured for Tertius to resume writing, his voice tight with emotion.

"You are trying to earn favor with God by observing certain days or months or seasons or years. I fear for you. Perhaps all my hard work with you was for nothing. Dear brothers and sisters, I plead with you to live as I do in freedom from these things, for I have become like you Gentiles—free from those laws" (4:10–12).

Paul's concern was palpable. Tertius paused for a moment, glancing up. Paul didn't notice—his gaze was distant, his thoughts focused entirely on the Galatians. His voice softened but did not lose its intensity. He continued dictating.

"You did not mistreat me when I first preached to you. Surely you remember that I was sick when I first brought you the Good News. But even though my condition tempted you to reject me, you did not despise me or turn me away. No, you took me in and cared for me as though I were an angel from God[2] or even Christ Jesus himself" (4:12–14).

As Tertius wrote, a question formed in his mind. "Sir, I wasn't there. May I ask: What happened in Galatia? You speak of illness, but it sounds like there's more to the story."

Paul closed his eyes, as if weighed down by the past. "Yes, Tertius. Let me tell you what happened."

CHAPTER 22

MY DEAR CHILDREN

(GALATIANS 4:15–20)

A SHADOW OF WEARINESS crossed Paul's face as memories surfaced.

"When I first began preaching in Galatia, I was a mess—bruised, broken, and weak. I had already faced opposition in Antioch and Iconium, but in Lystra, they didn't just oppose me—they stoned me and left me for dead. They thought they had finished me off. I can still feel the stones slamming into my body, my face…my eyes swollen shut from the blows."[1]

His hand moved absently to his head, as though he could still feel the pain there.

"You were stoned, sir?"

Paul's voice grew quieter, the memory drawing him inward. "Yes, they hurled stones at me, fully intent on killing me. Somehow God spared me, but my body was wrecked. My eyes…they were especially damaged. Swollen, disfigured. I could barely see. As I traveled through the other cities of Galatia, I was still recovering—my vision blurred; the dust from the road stung like fire in my eyes. They were severely swollen, with fluid dripping out of them. I was hideous to look at, and frankly, it was terribly embarrassing."

Paul continued, his tone now tinged with sadness.

"In this part of the Gentile world, there are so many

superstitions. Someone with damaged eyes was often feared. They called it the 'evil eye'—believing that a disfigured gaze could carry a curse. People would spit on the ground when they saw me, to ward off the curse, to protect themselves from misfortune.[2] It happened to me constantly. Mothers would pull their children away, shielding their eyes. It was humiliating."

His voice tightened, the vulnerability of that time clear in his words. "And the Judaizers used this against me, Tertius. They're Jews, like us—they don't even believe in these superstitions. But that didn't stop them from exploiting my condition. They whispered to the Galatians, planting seeds of doubt. 'Look at him,' they said. 'His eyes are cursed. He carries the evil eye, and if you follow him, you'll be cursed too.' They attacked my appearance, my weakness—anything to undermine the message I brought."

Tertius' frown deepened. "Sir, I had no idea."

Paul nodded gravely. "It would have been so easy for the Galatians to reject me, to spit at me like so many others did. But they didn't. Instead, they showed me mercy. They welcomed me into their homes, cared for my wounds, and ignored the whispers of the skeptics. They saw beyond the sickness, beyond my damaged eyes. They treated me as though I were an angel from God."

Paul's eyes glistened, the memory of their kindness moving his emotions. "That's why it cuts me so deeply now, to see how easily they're being led astray. They rejected the lies once. They refused to spit at me, refused to believe I carried the evil eye. But now it's as if they've forgotten all of that."

Tertius' eyes widened as realization struck. "Is that why you asked them who had cast the evil eye on them earlier?"[3]

"Good catch, Tertius. When they read, 'Who has cast an evil spell on you?,' they will know exactly what I'm talking about. The Judaizers accused me of carrying a curse, but it's they who are poisoning the Galatians with their lies. They called me the curse-bearer, but in reality they're the ones bringing the law's curse back upon the Galatians."

Paul paced the room now, his urgency growing with every word. "That's what makes it so tragic. The very ones who were set free by the gospel are being led back into chains—chains of fear." A tear rolled down his face as he pressed on, dictating more slowly now.

"Where is that joyful and grateful spirit you felt then? I am sure you would have taken out your own eyes and given them to me if it had been possible. Have I now become your enemy because I am telling you the truth?" (4:15–16).

Paul wiped the tear from his face and turned his back to Tertius, clearly trying to hide his emotion. Sitting on the corner of the table, he continued to dictate.

"Those false teachers are so eager to win your favor, but their intentions are not good. They are trying to shut you off from me so that you will pay attention only to them. If someone is eager to do good things for you, that's all right; but let them do it all the time, not just when I'm with you!" (4:17–18).

Tertius finished writing, then glanced at Paul, brow furrowed. "Sir, these false teachers…why do they hate you so much? I understand that they disagree with you, but this feels personal."

Paul turned slightly, his eyes meeting Tertius' with a look of quiet frustration.

"Their goal is to separate the Galatians from me completely—cutting them off from the truth I taught them. If they succeed, the Galatians will no longer listen to me, no longer trust what I've said. Instead, they'll become dependent on these false teachers."

"Ah, so it's about control?"

"Yes! They're positioning themselves as the gatekeepers of the kingdom, setting conditions that Christ Himself never set. They're withholding access to table fellowship—refusing to eat with the Galatians because they haven't met their legalistic demands. This isn't just exclusion; it's manipulation. These false teachers want the Galatians to believe they're on the outside, looking in—locked out from the people of God until they submit to their demands."

Paul began pacing again, his frustration giving way to a heavy sadness that weighed on his heart like a grieving father. The Galatians—his spiritual children, whom he had nurtured with love and truth—were being led astray. But it was worse than that. The very ones who were abusing and manipulating them had twisted their minds so thoroughly that they now saw Paul, their true protector, as the enemy.

The abusers had convinced the children that the father who loved them was the real threat. And now, in their confusion, they were pushing away the one who would give anything to save them, embracing instead the very hands that bound them.

He shook his head, battling a tide of emotions, his voice tinged with fatherly sorrow.

"Keep writing, Tertius. **'Oh, my dear children! I feel as if I'm going through labor pains for you again, and they will continue until Christ is fully developed in your lives. I wish I were with you right now so I could change my tone. But at this distance I don't know how else to help you'**" (4:19–20).

As Tertius finished writing, he noticed Paul staring out the window again, profound sadness in his eyes. The Galatians weren't just converts to him—they were his spiritual children, and the thought of them turning away from the truth cut him deeply.

CHAPTER 23

WHO IS YOUR MOTHER?

(GALATIANS 4:21–5:1)

THE AFTERNOON SUNLIGHT filled the room as Paul, still standing, reached for the next shard of the broken jar. His fingers traced its edges, his lips pressed together in concentration as he studied the writing scrawled across its surface. Paul's voice broke the silence as he read aloud, **"Hagar: Law, Sarah: Promise."**

Tertius looked up. "Hagar and Sarah? What do they have to do with the Galatians?"

Paul kept turning the shard in his fingers, then looked up, a smile forming on his face.

"You remember the story of Sarah and Hagar, don't you?"

"Yes, sir," Tertius replied, clearing his throat. "Of course I do."

Paul knew Tertius had heard the story countless times. But he wanted him to see it as never before.

"Picture the scene, Tertius," he began. "Sarah had heard God's promise—descendants as numerous as the stars—but as the years passed, her body weakened and her hope dimmed. In her desperation, Sarah took matters into her own hands. She brought her servant, Hagar, to Abraham. It's an uncomfortable story, isn't it?"

Tertius smiled, a bit embarrassed. "Now that you mention it, yes. I always thought it was just me."

Paul laughed softly. "Oh, it's awkward, all right. Hagar, a young servant girl, suddenly carrying an eighty-six-year-old man's child?[1] And not just any child—Abraham's heir. They were trying to fulfill God's promise by themselves. But things didn't go as planned, did they? Hagar's pregnancy stirred something dark in Sarah—jealousy, bitterness. Sarah grew angry, feeling like what was meant to be hers had now been given to Hagar. And Hagar? How do you think she felt?"

After a moment of contemplation, Tertius replied. "She must have felt proud, maybe even powerful, knowing she was carrying Abraham's son."

Paul nodded. "She began looking down on Sarah. The tension between them grew until it became unbearable. Sarah mistreated Hagar so badly that she fled into the desert—remember? Can you picture it? Hagar, alone and pregnant, wandering the wilderness with no one. But then God stepped in.[2] The angel told Hagar to return, promising that her son would become a great nation too.[3] She obeyed. Ishmael was born. And things seemed to settle down."

Tertius smiled. "Until Isaac was born, right?"

"Exactly. After years—fourteen years!—Sarah finally gave birth.[4] And it wasn't just any birth. Sarah was ninety, Abraham a hundred. Isaac's birth was nothing short of supernatural—a gift from God."

Paul leaned in. "Now imagine the household. Isaac, the child of promise, growing up, carrying the legacy of God's covenant. But Ishmael, the son of human effort, begins mocking him. The jealousy between Sarah and Hagar passed down to their sons, and Sarah saw it."

Tertius leaned back in his chair, fingers steepled near his mouth as he pondered. The story was familiar, but he was eager to see where Paul would take it next.

"Sarah knew they couldn't live side by side," Paul said. "She realized Ishmael would never share Isaac's inheritance, so she urged Abraham to send them away.[5] Abraham was torn—he loved Ishmael. But the promise belonged to Isaac. Hagar and Ishmael had to leave.

Now the Judaizers are twisting that very story. They claim that only those under the law are true heirs, like Isaac, and that anyone who refuses to submit is like Ishmael—cast out from the promise."

Paul's eyes narrowed, sharp and focused. "But I'm about to turn the tables on them."

Tertius leaned forward, intrigued by the shift in Paul's tone. "How will you do that, sir?"

Paul studied the shard in his hand. "Well, Tertius, Abraham had two sons. Yes, two. And the real question is—which one do they *really* resemble?"

He set the shard aside, and Tertius picked up his pen.

"Write this," Paul said. **"Tell me, you who want to live under the law, do you know what the law actually says? The Scriptures say that Abraham had two sons, one from his slave wife and one from his freeborn wife. The son of the slave wife was born in a human attempt to bring about the fulfillment of God's promise. But the son of the freeborn wife was born as God's own fulfillment of his promise. These two women serve as an illustration of God's two covenants. The first woman, Hagar, represents Mount Sinai where people received the law that enslaved them. And now Jerusalem is just like Mount Sinai in Arabia, because she and her children live in slavery to the law. But the other woman, Sarah, represents the heavenly Jerusalem. She is the free woman, and she is our mother"** (4:21–26).

Tertius wrote quickly but paused at the final line.

"Hold on," he said. "What is the 'heavenly Jerusalem'?"

Paul's eyes brightened. "Ah, Tertius, I thought that might get your attention. Jerusalem and Sinai—these places mean so much to us as Jews, don't they? Many still pray, bowing toward Jerusalem, as though the city itself is God's dwelling place. But what I'm talking about is a new home for the new people of God. It's the city Abraham was looking for—a city not built with physical stones or human hands, a city built by God Himself. It's not just a future hope. It's here, in Christ, right now. Anyone who would cease from his own works and trust fully in Christ can live there—in true freedom."

Tertius leaned back. "What about Jerusalem here on earth? Does it not matter anymore?"

"The physical Jerusalem—what it once stood for—has changed," Paul said. "It's a city that turned its back on its own Messiah. It became consumed by pride and corruption, trapped in rituals that no longer bring life. God's presence no longer dwells behind that curtain in the temple. It's a city blind and bound by religion. No, Tertius. That's not our home anymore."

Paul continued. "We have a new home now—a city of rest for the people of God. A place where the Sabbath is not just a day but a way of life. It is the fulfillment of what our Lord Himself said: 'Come to Me, all you who labor and are heavy laden, and I will give you rest.' No endless sacrifices. No bondage. No sin. No curse. There is no need for a physical temple. We are the temple—God dwells among His people! It is not bound to Sinai, not tethered to the old Jerusalem, still toiling under the weight of the law. No, this is the Jerusalem above—the mother of all who believe. The city of promise. The inheritance of those who trust, who cease from their own works and rest in Christ alone."

Tertius' gaze drifted as he basked in Paul's words. He sat with them for a moment, savoring their weight, their wonder. But even as he marveled, a question tugged at the edge of his thoughts, like a thread left untied.

"But what does it mean that this heavenly Jerusalem is our mother?"

"We just wrote it," Paul said. "Sarah represents the heavenly Jerusalem in our analogy."

Tertius brought a finger to his lips, scanning the parchment. "And...Hagar represents Sinai and the earthly Jerusalem?"

Paul gave a firm nod. "Good. Now tell me, what do Hagar, Sinai, and the earthly Jerusalem have in common?"

"Well...according to your analogy, I suppose they all represent bondage," he said, almost thinking aloud. "Hagar was a slave. Sinai gave the law, which binds us. And Jerusalem—the earthly Jerusalem—is still in slavery under the law."

Paul held his gaze. "By the way, where did Hagar go when she was cast out?"

Tertius hesitated. "Into the wilderness?"

"Yes. The desert of Paran—the very region of Sinai, where the law was given."

Paul crossed his arms, watching the realization wash over his scribe. "But now let's talk about Sarah. What does she represent?"

Tertius answered softly, "Freedom."

"Exactly. Sarah was free—and so is the heavenly Jerusalem. A city of promise, not bound by the law. And that is exactly why those who belong to Christ are children of the free woman, not the slave."

Tertius' mouth parted slightly, his eyes lifting as the connection clicked into place.

"But there's more," Paul said. "Think about it—when Isaac, the true heir, was born, Ishmael had to go. And now that Christ, the fulfillment of the promise, has come, the law has done its job. It's time to let it go. Here's the point, Tertius—Hagar was a slave, and so are those who rely on the law. Her son didn't inherit the promise, and neither do those under the law.

"This is the exact opposite of what the Judaizers teach. They claim obeying the law makes someone a true heir, like Isaac. But in truth, they're more like Ishmael—born through human striving, still in slavery. It's faith, not law-keeping, that makes us children of the promise."

Tertius paused, tapping his pen against the parchment. "So

the Galatian Gentiles are the real children of Sarah? That's a bold take."

Paul raised his finger, a firm correction in his voice.

"It's those who put their faith in *Christ* that are the children of Sarah—the children of promise—Jew or Gentile makes no difference."

Tertius sat back, blinking as new categories began to form in his mind.

Paul picked up the shard again, the inscription "Hagar: Law, Sarah: Promise" tethering his thoughts to the gospel.

"Write this: **'As Isaiah said, "Rejoice, O childless woman, you who have never given birth! Break into a joyful shout, you who have never been in labor! For the desolate woman now has more children than the woman who lives with her husband." And you, dear brothers and sisters, are children of the promise, just like Isaac'**" (4:27–28).[6]

Tertius wrote as Paul spoke, his mind turning over the familiar Isaiah passage—a prophecy of restoration. But Paul wasn't just quoting it; he was applying it in a radical new way.

The barren woman, once seen as Zion longing for restoration, now pointed to Sarah—the mother of promise. And her miraculous children weren't just the descendants of Isaac, but all who put their faith in Christ, Jews and Gentiles alike. Once outsiders to the covenant, they were now heirs, part of God's family by faith, citizens of the new heavenly Jerusalem.

Paul returned to the table under the window, dipping a finger into the pot of resin. "But Tertius, you need to understand something. Ishmaels will always persecute Isaacs. Those born according to the flesh will always persecute those born by the Spirit. That's exactly what the Judaizers are doing to the Galatians."

Paul applied the adhesive, his fingers tracing the jagged edge with precision. "Write this: **'But you are now being persecuted by those who want you to keep the law, just as Ishmael, the**

child born by human effort, persecuted Isaac, the child born by the power of the Spirit'" (4:29).[7]

Tertius grinned as he wrote, the genius of Paul's insight becoming clearer. "What an observation, sir. You're so right—the Judaizers are acting like Ishmael, bullying and manipulating the Galatians!"

Paul nodded grimly, stepping back to examine the jar. "Yes. And they've twisted everything to make it look as though they're the true heirs. But in reality, they are just like Ishmael."

He continued, "Write this: **'But what do the Scriptures say about that? "Get rid of the slave and her son, for the son of the slave woman will not share the inheritance with the free woman's son." So, dear brothers and sisters, we are not children of the slave woman; we are children of the free woman'"** (4:30–31).[8]

"The Judaizers have tried to convince the Galatians that circumcision will make them part of the family, like Ishmael. But that's not how it works. Only the children of the promise inherit the promise. And circumcision doesn't bring that inheritance—faith does."

Tertius finished writing. He watched Paul intently, the jar now taking on a more complete shape, though the cracks and scars still ran through it. Paul stepped back, examining it from every angle.

"We're free, Tertius," he said softly, his eyes lingering on the jar. "We're Sarah's children, citizens of the heavenly Jerusalem. The promise is ours—that's what Jesus did for us! Incredible, isn't it?"

Tertius pressed a hand to his heart. "Amazing, sir."

Paul turned to him, his expression serious. "But Tertius, we've got to stay free. We can never go back to that old bondage. Not for a moment."

"Do you want me to write that, sir?" Tertius asked, more a suggestion than a question.

"Yes! Absolutely," Paul said. "Write this, **'So Christ has truly set us free. Now make sure that you stay free, and don't get tied up again in slavery to the law'**" (5:1).

CHAPTER 24

BACK INTO BONDAGE

(GALATIANS 5:2–3)

PAUL REACHED FOR the next shard of the broken jar. He read aloud the note he had written to himself, **"Circumcision: Cut Off from Christ."**

Before Tertius could ask a question, there was a sudden knock at the door.

Both men turned, startled by the interruption. The door creaked open. Gaius, their host, entered. In his hands, he carried a wooden tray laden with bread and fruit—figs, grapes, and dates—a testament to his thoughtful hospitality.

A young servant followed close behind, his movements quick and efficient. He carried a large pitcher brimming with water.

"Paul, it's been hours. I thought you might need a break," Gaius said with a warm smile. "I didn't think you'd still be working so late in the afternoon."

Paul returned Gaius' smile. "Your timing is perfect as always, my friend. Please, come in."

Gaius stepped into the room, setting the tray down on the bench by the door. He looked at Tertius and nodded. "Looks like everything's going well in here."

"It's been smooth so far," Tertius said. "Paul's insights never fail to amaze."

Paul clapped Gaius on the shoulder. "Gaius, you have the heart of a true host. Your kindness is a gift to us all."

Gaius waved off the compliment. "It's the least I can do." He glanced at the table, his eyes focusing on the broken pottery. "What's all this about?" He gestured to the scattered shards and the nearly reconstructed jar.

Paul held a touch of mystery in his expression. "It's…a reminder," he said.

Gaius raised an eyebrow, his lips curling into a knowing smile. He was used to Paul's penchant for drama and mystery but didn't press further. "Well, I'll leave you to your work." He clasped Paul's hand with a firm shake.

Tertius nodded gratefully. "Thank you, sir."

Gaius gave a final nod and left the room, the servant trailing behind him. As the door clicked shut, the room fell back into a comfortable silence. Tertius stood, the visit from Gaius reminding him to stretch his legs. He made his way to the table with the refreshments, pouring a cup of water for Paul before filling one for himself.

"Now, where were we?" Paul said.

Tertius looked down at the shard in Paul's other hand. "You just read it aloud—'Circumcision: Cut Off from Christ.'"

Paul turned the shard over in his fingers, nodding. "Ah, yes." He exhaled, then met Tertius' gaze with a steady look. "Let's get down to business."

Tertius returned to the table and sat down with purpose, knowing that whatever came next would be crucial.

"The real danger, Tertius, isn't just theological confusion. The Galatians aren't simply debating ideas—they're standing at the edge of a cliff, about to make a decision that will sever their relationship with Christ completely."

Paul placed the water cup back on the table and moved across the room, toward the half-restored jar under the window.

With careful hands, he began applying resin to the edge of the shard he was holding. "They've been convinced by the Judaizers that faith isn't enough. They're being led to believe that circumcision will make them part of God's people."

Tertius tilted his head slightly, a hint of perplexity crossing his face. "But didn't we cover this already, sir?"

Paul's expression darkened, his voice taking on a sharper edge. "Oh, Tertius, we've barely scratched the surface on this. Now we're getting to the heart of it: They don't realize that turning to circumcision doesn't just bring them under a ritual—it puts them under the whole law. This isn't just about adding a harmless custom. The Judaizers are telling them to bind themselves to the law. But once they take that first step, they're obligated to keep all 613 commandments—every rule, every regulation, every sacrifice."

Paul's frustration was palpable as he continued. "Do they really understand what they're getting themselves into? They'll have to observe every dietary law, remember every festival, never break the Sabbath—not even once! And what about the sacrifices? Are they ready to bring lambs, goats, and bulls to the temple for every sin? Ready to keep tassels on their cloaks, refuse shellfish, and scour their homes for leaven before Passover?"

His hands stilled, his voice thick with urgency. "If they fail to keep just one—one!—of these 613 laws, they'll be guilty of breaking the entire law. And then what? They'll be shackled to an impossible standard, crushed under a burden no one can bear."

Tertius, listening intently, shook his head as the reality of the situation sank in. "It's impossible," he said quietly.

Paul's eyes flashed with indignation. "Absolutely! And we know it, Tertius. We were born into this—raised under its crushing demands.[1] But we were set free! We proclaimed that glorious freedom to the world. And now these Gentiles, who were never even bound to the law, are walking straight into it, on purpose! They think they're gaining righteousness, but what they're really gaining is a new kind of bondage. It's not righteousness they're adding—it's chains. And no matter how hard they try, it'll never be enough."

Paul's pace quickened as he dictated the next part. **"Listen! I, Paul, tell you this: If you are counting on circumcision to make you right with God, then Christ will be of no benefit to you. I'll say it again: If you are trying to find favor with God by being circumcised, you must obey every regulation in the whole law of Moses"** (5:2–3).

CHAPTER 25

CUT OFF FROM CHRIST

(GALATIANS 5:4–6)

PAUL'S EXPRESSION SOFTENED. He paused, his eyes distant for a moment before turning back to Tertius. "Remember how God delivered our ancestors from Egypt—performing unprecedented miracles to crush the mightiest empire on earth and set them free? And yet in the wilderness, when they faced hardship, what did they do? They wanted to go back! They missed the comfort of familiarity—the leeks, the garlic, the false sense of security they felt under their old chains."

Tertius nodded, following Paul's line of thought.

"No power on earth could drag them back into slavery, Tertius, yet they nearly walked back to Egypt by their own choice! And now the Galatians are doing the very same thing. They were freed from every kind of bondage—spiritual slavery—and it was glorious. When Jesus sets someone free, they are utterly and completely free. All the powers of darkness combined could not force them back into chains.

"But what if they choose to return? What if they long for the false sense of security and comfort they once had in Egypt? That's why I said earlier, **'Christ has truly set us free. Now make sure that you stay free, and don't get tied up again in slavery to the law'**" (5:1).

Paul continued working on the jar. The adhesive now applied, he carefully pressed the shard into place. His fingers slipped. A sharp sting—the jagged edge slicing into his skin. He sucked in a breath, instinctively bringing the cut to his mouth as the shard tumbled onto the table.

Tertius glanced up. "Paul—your hand."

Without responding, Paul pressed his finger into the palm of his other hand, gazing at the cut as though seeing the Galatians' plight reflected in the wound. His voice broke the silence.

"They think it's just a small cut? A simple snip of flesh to somehow make them holier? No, they're doing far more. They're cutting themselves off from Christ—severing their entire souls from the very source of life." His eyes darkened as he continued. "They believe this act will bring them closer to God? They might as well be holding the knife against their own throats. It's not just foreskin they're cutting off; it's their bond with Christ. They're not just trimming flesh; they're amputating their lifeline to grace. They'll end up like a branch hacked off from the vine, tossed aside to wither and die—completely disconnected from the life that only Christ can give.

"Do you see what they're doing, Tertius? When they placed their faith in Christ, they severed themselves from bondage to belong to Him.[1] Now they are severing themselves from Christ to return to that same bondage.[2] They're undoing their own deliverance!"

He looked up, his voice thick with frustration. "Write this: **'For if you are trying to make yourselves right with God by keeping the law, you have been cut off from Christ! You have fallen away from God's grace'**" (5:4).

Tertius dipped his reed pen in ink, his lips a thin line as he recorded Paul's words. The severity of the statement hung in the air like a judgment.

"So if they do this…they won't even be considered believers anymore? They'll be completely cut off—from Christ, from the church?"

Paul nodded. "It's absolutely that serious. Apostasy has always been a danger to God's people. Ezekiel warned that if the righteous turn away, their former righteousness will be forgotten.[3] Circumcision itself isn't sin—but relying on it is turning away from the only remedy for sin. If they take this path, their past sins won't be atoned for, because true atonement comes through the blood of Jesus, not the blood of circumcision."

Paul turned back to the jar. Picking up the shard that had fallen, he pressed it into place with deliberate care. A small smear of blood from his cut lingered on the pottery's edge, mingling with the cracks and imperfections. The jar was taking shape, its scars more visible with each piece fitted together, a silent testament to the wounds of both the vessel and its mender.

Paul waited, listening for Tertius to finish writing. His gaze drifted back to his finger. Without looking up, he continued dictating. **"But we who live by the Spirit eagerly wait to receive by faith the righteousness God has promised to us. For when we place our faith in Christ Jesus, there is no benefit in being circumcised or being uncircumcised. What is important is faith expressing itself in love"** (5:5–6).

Paul continued. "The law binds, Tertius. But the Spirit sets us free. The Galatians think they can somehow ensure their salvation by keeping the law, but in doing so they're shackling themselves to a system no one can fulfill. What matters is not the law but faith—faith that naturally expresses itself in love."

CHAPTER 26

MUTILATING THE FLESH

(GALATIANS 5:7–12)

PAUL STOOD BY the window, the half-restored jar on the table forgotten for the moment. His movements grew sharper, more animated, as his gaze locked on Tertius with a renewed sense of urgency.

He began pacing, the sound of his sandals scuffing lightly against the floor. "Write this: **'You were running the race so well. Who has held you back from following the truth? It certainly isn't God, for he is the one who called you to freedom. This false teaching is like a little yeast that spreads through the whole batch of dough!'**" (5:7–9).[1]

Tertius paused, finishing the last words on the parchment before glancing up. "Sir, this imagery feels familiar. Didn't Jesus also speak about yeast?"

"Absolutely," Paul said. "Jesus warned us about the yeast of the Pharisees—referring to their teaching, which was laced with hypocrisy and legalism."[2]

He reached for the tray of refreshments Gaius had brought earlier, his fingers closing around a rustic loaf of bread. As he tore off a small piece, the smell of fresh bread mingled with the sweet scent of figs.

"And just like with them," Paul continued, "a little yeast from these Judaizers can corrupt everything. Once it spreads, it can't be undone. The dough is permanently changed." He glanced down at the loaf in his hands, his expression tightening. "Once it rises, there's no going back."

He set the rest of the loaf back on the tray, still holding the torn piece.

Tertius nodded slowly, the vivid imagery sinking in.

"This is why I'm so alarmed," Paul said. "If this false teaching isn't dealt with, it won't just harm a few churches in Galatia—it'll spread like yeast through the entire church. What starts as a small distortion will eventually corrupt the gospel itself. Future generations will inherit a twisted version of the truth, tainted with legalism."

Tertius stared back, his eyes wide with concern.

"But we know how to deal with leaven,[3] don't we?" Paul said. "What do we do with it every year before Passover, to celebrate the Feast of Unleavened Bread?"

Tertius straightened, recognizing the allusion. "We search it out. We remove every last crumb of leaven from our homes. We sweep the corners, clean every surface, and burn whatever remains."

"Right! It's a complete purging to ensure no trace is left behind. And that's what we must do now with this false teaching. It's not enough to refute it—we must eradicate it completely. If even a little remains, it could spread and corrupt the whole church."

Paul tore off a piece of the bread in his hand and placed it in his mouth, chewing thoughtfully. Tertius sat in silence, absorbing the gravity of the situation. This wasn't just about correcting a misunderstanding—it was about protecting the future of the gospel itself.

After a moment, Tertius voiced a fresh concern.

"But sir, the leaven isn't just hidden. It's being spread—on purpose. If the false teaching is intentional, and spreading everywhere, what hope do we have of stopping it?"

Paul swallowed and straightened. "The good news, Tertius, is that Jesus promised He would build His own church. I'm confident that the true church will not be corrupted or destroyed. But woe to those false teachers who are sowing confusion. Their judgment will come, and the truth will stand. Write this: **'I am trusting the Lord to keep you from believing false teachings. God will judge that person, whoever he is, who has been confusing you'"** (5:10).

Tertius scribbled the words, glancing up to see Paul's face set with righteous anger.

"Dear brothers and sisters," he continued, **"if I were still preaching that you must be circumcised—as some say I do[4]—why am I still being persecuted? If I were no longer preaching salvation through the cross of Christ, no one would be offended"** (5:11).

The tension in the room grew thicker, and Paul's frustration boiled over.

"And these Judaizers—so eager to mutilate flesh..." Paul's voice rose, simmering with fury. "If they love their blades so much, I wish their hand would slip and take the whole thing off! Why stop at the foreskin? Let them castrate themselves completely and be done with it!"

Tertius froze, his reed pen hovering over the parchment in the awkward silence.

"Write it," Paul commanded, pointing to the parchment.

Tertius swallowed hard, unsure. The words hung in the air, raw and biting—sharper than anything he ever expected to hear from Paul.

"Sir, are you sure about this?" he asked. "It sounds like anger. Like you're lashing out."

Paul turned sharply, eyes flashing. "Yes, Tertius. I'm sure."

Tertius glanced from the reed pen to Paul, searching for any sign of reconsideration.

Paul's intense gaze didn't waver, but his expression softened as he stepped closer to the table.

"Listen, I know it's strong. But I'm not lashing out. I want them to feel the emotion, yes! But when the shock of the statement fades, they'll see there's more to it—layers of meaning. Trust me."

Tertius sighed quietly. He would write what he was told, but a part of him wondered if Paul's passion had blurred the line. If there were layers of meaning, he couldn't see them.

Paul didn't owe Tertius an explanation, but he didn't want to leave his brother burdened by doubt either. He leaned in, with a hint of a smile.

"For the Judaizers, the ones who cling to the law, this will hit them hard. They know the Torah, Tertius. They know Deuteronomy 23. If a man mutilates himself, if he cuts off his private parts, he's cut off from the assembly of God.[5] So they'd never openly promote mutilation, but by insisting on circumcision as a means of righteousness, they're stepping closer than they realize. They're blind to where this path leads—and the Torah itself warns them."

Tertius blinked, realization dawning in his eyes. Maybe Paul really did have a constructive point to make.

Paul popped the rest of the torn bread into his mouth, chewing thoughtfully as a pause settled between them.

"And the Gentiles," he continued, "for them castration is tied to the pagan rituals they've left behind. In Galatia, everyone knows about the Galli—the priests of Cybele. These men, in their frenzied state, driven by wild music and chanting, work themselves into a madness during their festivals. At the height of their frenzy, they take blades and castrate themselves as an offering to 'the mother goddess.' It's a spectacle—bloody and grotesque. They throw their severed genitals into the crowd as part of the ritual."

Tertius winced, the horror of it sinking in. He hadn't realized it was that extreme.

"The Romans themselves find it barbaric," Paul continued, "so much so that they refused to let eunuchs serve as priests when they adopted Cybele's cult. The Galli are despised, mocked, seen as men who've mutilated themselves for nothing. And yet these Judaizers, pushing circumcision, are luring the Galatians right back into the kind of ritualistic mutilation they thought they had escaped. So when I say I wish they'd go all the way and castrate themselves, I'm not just being crude. I'm showing them the path they're walking—the same bondage they left behind in their paganism."

Tertius sat back, eyes wide, half smiling. Paul's statement wasn't just sharp, it was surgical—a genius maneuver in the argument.

Paul continued. "They need to feel this, Tertius. If they don't grasp the severity, they'll walk willingly into slavery. And I won't stand by and let that happen."

With a steady hand, Tertius dipped the reed pen once more.

"Could you say it again, sir? I want to write it exactly the way you mean."

Paul's gaze was unyielding. **"I just wish that those troublemakers who want to mutilate you by circumcision would mutilate themselves!"** (5:12).

Tertius swallowed and wrote the words. Even though the tone clashed with his own temperament, he knew Paul was right. In moments like these, Tertius was thankful his name wouldn't be on the letter.

CHAPTER 27

FREE TO SERVE

(GALATIANS 5:13–15)

PAUL," TERTIUS SAID, his voice cutting through the stillness of the late afternoon, "only two pieces left! You're almost there!"

The sun, beginning its descent, cast long shadows across the table, illuminating the nearly completed jar. The once-shattered vessel stood tall, its wildflower motifs and fractured body pieced together with care and intention. Two crucial shards remained, each bearing words Paul had etched into them weeks earlier.

Paul paused, reached for the second-to-last fragment, and ran a hand through his graying hair. The weariness of the long day was evident, but a glint of purpose still shone in his eyes. He smiled at Tertius' enthusiasm but remained contemplative.

Tertius's gaze lingered on the jar, the metaphor becoming clearer with every piece. "The most intricate shards are at the top," he observed quietly. "They pull it all together."

Paul's hands remained steady as he held the fragment, despite the long hours behind them.

"That's right, Tertius. The final parts are extremely important. We've covered a lot of ground today, but we can't let up now. These last pieces…they're not just the top—they're the crown. Everything has been building toward this."

Tertius watched Paul's face, sensing the depth of his words—he was speaking about much more than the jar.

Paul met his gaze. "Stay sharp. I know we're tired, but this is the part that matters most. I've saved the best for last." He turned the shard over, as if recalling the moment he had first inscribed it. He paused, then read the words of the heading aloud: **"Walk by the Spirit."** After a moment, he set it down again.

"Tertius, before we move on, I want to hear what you've taken from all this. What have you heard me say about the gospel versus the law so far?"

Tertius cleared his throat before responding. "You've taught that we are no longer under the burden of the law. The gospel frees us because Christ fulfilled the law for us. Circumcision, festivals, dietary restrictions—none of these can make us righteous. Only faith in Christ justifies us."

Paul nodded. "Go on."

Tertius continued, "And you've said that the law enslaves while the gospel brings freedom. The law shows us our sin, but it can't save us. It only condemns. The gospel, on the other hand, offers salvation by grace, through faith—not by works."

Paul smiled, clearly pleased with Tertius' understanding. "Yes, you've heard correctly. That is all true." He paused, then leaned forward slightly, locking eyes with Tertius. "But there's something more—something crucial that you've missed."

Tertius frowned, uncertain of what he had overlooked.

"You've described the freedom from the law accurately, but you're forgetting a key part of this freedom. It's not just freedom *from* the law; it's freedom *for* something. The gospel doesn't release us from the law's demands and leave us wandering without direction. It replaces the external rules of the law with the indwelling power of the Holy Spirit."

Tertius brought his hand to his forehead. "Of course! The Spirit! How could I forget?" He shook his head, frustrated with himself.

Paul chuckled softly. "Don't forget that, Tertius. It's not irrelevant. Without the Spirit, none of this works! Remember when we talked about the way Jesus sent the Holy Spirit on the day of Pentecost?"

Tertius nodded, recalling the vivid description Paul had shared.

"The outpouring of the Spirit wasn't just some afterthought—it was the very promise of God, the fulfillment of everything the prophets longed for. The Holy Spirit is the heart of it all. Without Him, we're left with dead rituals, powerless to change us from the inside. But with Him, we're transformed. The Galatians need to grasp this too. We're free from the law, yes, but not free to do whatever we want. We're free to walk in step with the Spirit, to live by His power, and that changes everything."

Tertius stared at Paul, a look of amazement crossing his face. Everything Paul had said, as disjointed as it may have felt previously, was now connecting like pieces in an elaborate puzzle.

"Yes! The Spirit brings everything together. It's wonderful," Tertius said, his eyes shifting to the jar on the table under the window.

Paul saw the recognition in the scribe's eyes.

"I'm glad you're seeing it, Tertius. Without the Spirit, freedom would just be lawlessness. Some people twist my words to suggest that I'm encouraging chaos. But that's far from the truth. The Spirit enables us to obey God from the heart, driven by love, not fear of punishment. This freedom we have in Christ empowers us to live a life of obedience, not rebellion."

Tertius sat in silence, reflecting on Paul's words.

Paul continued. "This is the heart of the gospel: We are no longer slaves to the law, but neither are we slaves to sin. We are led by the Spirit, and it's the Spirit who produces in us the kind of life the law was always pointing to.

"Write this," Paul said, his voice firm. **"For you have been called to live in freedom, my brothers and sisters. But don't use your freedom to satisfy your [flesh].[1] Instead, use your freedom**

to serve one another in love. For the whole law can be summed up in this one command: 'Love your neighbor as yourself.' But if you are always biting and devouring one another, watch out! Beware of destroying one another" (5:13–15).[2]

Tertius dipped his reed pen into the ink pot and began writing, the sharp scratch of the pen cutting through the still air. When he finished, he glanced up.

"This is excellent, sir. I think this gets to the heart of the Judaizers' concern. They fear that without the law, everything will unravel—that people will fall into sin, division, and disorder."

Paul's eyes flashed as he leaned in, resting his hands on the table. "That's the very misunderstanding I've been warning against, Tertius," he said, shaking his head. "They think it's the law that keeps people in line."

Paul began pacing as he gathered his thoughts.

"But here's the irony—the ones warning of chaos are the ones causing it! And they're using the law to do it! They stir up division, suspicion, and control—all in the name of righteousness. But true righteousness doesn't come from the flesh, and it never will. It only comes when people walk in the Spirit."

Tertius furrowed his brow. "Sir, you keep referring to 'the flesh.' Are you talking about circumcision—the cutting of flesh?"

Paul gave a dry chuckle, shaking his head. "Well, foreskin is certainly flesh, and the Judaizers insist that cutting it away makes a man righteous—so in a sense, yes, they have a literal flesh-based righteousness. But I mean something much deeper than that. I'm using wordplay to show that trusting in human effort for righteousness is, in the broader sense, also 'walking in the flesh.' Flesh is temporary, corruptible, dying. The Spirit is eternal, life-giving. To walk by the flesh is to rely on human strength—on effort, on externals. And that's why being under the law is walking according to the flesh.

"The law itself is good and spiritual[3]—but trusting in it for righteousness is still trusting in the flesh. Because at the end of the day, it's human effort. It's something external. And it's powerless to bring life. The flesh can never produce what only the Spirit can."

Paul tapped the table for emphasis. "And like the literal flesh on your body, the flesh is self-focused. It's self-reliant. That's why a life driven by the flesh always leads to division—because the flesh is always about self. Sooner or later, people start striving against each other. They compete. They dominate. They tear each other down. That's why wherever people walk in the flesh, you see jealousy, envy, strife.

"But the Spirit?" Paul lifted a hand slightly, as if grasping at something unseen. "The Spirit produces love, joy, peace—the very things the flesh could never produce. That's why walking by the Spirit isn't just another way to please God—it's the only way."[4]

Paul straightened, his voice soft now but still charged with conviction.

"And here's the irony the Judaizers will never understand: The ones trying the hardest to fulfill the law are the very ones breaking it. Why? Because love is the fulfillment of the law. And only the Spirit can produce love. Even some of our own sages teach that love is the totality of the law.[5] If we live in love for one another, we will never break the law. And the Spirit of God is the Spirit of love. If we are filled with the Spirit, we will walk in love."

Paul exhaled, shaking his head. "If only they could see it."

CHAPTER 28

WALK IN THE SPIRIT

(GALATIANS 5:16–18)

PAUL TURNED BACK toward the table where the shard bearing the words "Walk by the Spirit" lay, waiting for its place in the nearly restored jar. He picked it up gently, turning it over in his hands. There was a meaning behind the simple phrase that Paul seemed to contemplate intensely.

"Write this," Paul said, still focused on the shard. **"So I say, let the Holy Spirit guide your lives. Then you won't be doing what your [flesh] craves"** (5:16).

He set the shard down, its weathered glaze resting against the table. Its jagged edge, raw and exposed, awaited the resin.

"I hope you can see it now, Tertius. It's the Spirit that makes all the difference. We're not talking about throwing away the law and doing whatever we want. That would lead to chaos. Without the Spirit, they'll fall back into sin, into indulgence. But with Him—when they walk in the Spirit—they'll not only meet the law's demands, they'll surpass them."

"But what about temptation?" Tertius asked. "Won't they still struggle with sin?"

Paul's gaze drifted toward the dimming light outside. He sighed.

"Tertius, there is a war inside every believer, and it won't stop until the day we leave these bodies behind. But that's precisely why we need the Spirit. The Spirit empowers us to fight back. Without Him, we'd stumble, fall, and fail. But with the Spirit, we are more than conquerors.

"Write this: **'The flesh wants to do evil, which is just the opposite of what the Spirit wants. And the Spirit gives us desires that are the opposite of what the [flesh] desires. These two forces are constantly fighting each other, so you are not free to carry out your good intentions. But when you are directed by the Spirit, you are not under obligation to the law of Moses'"** (5:17–18).

As Tertius wrote, Paul returned to the jar and applied the sticky resin to the jagged edges of the shard. The inside curve of the shard bore the words "Walk by the Spirit," etched in Paul's bold, large letters. He pressed the piece into place with deliberate care.

Tertius glanced up from the parchment, his eyes tracing the nearly completed jar. Its delicate wildflower pattern curled up toward the ornate rim, with just one final piece waiting to be placed.

"Sir?" His voice was hesitant, a question clearly weighing on him.

Paul looked up, rubbing the sticky resin off his hands. "Yes, Tertius?"

"You mentioned that the Spirit gives us good desires that oppose the desires of the flesh. But you said it's a fight that rages in every believer. Is that right?"

Paul nodded. "Yes, that's true."

Tertius carefully considered his next words. "So…even *you* still struggle with your flesh?"

A small smile pulled at Paul's lips, disarming in its honesty. "Of course. I'm human just like you. As long as we live in these bodies, the struggle remains."

Tertius exhaled softly, a mix of relief and disappointment washing over his face.

"However," Paul added, stepping back to inspect the nearly completed jar, "we are in a totally different situation now. Once, we were trapped, struggling in our own strength, striving to follow rules that could never truly change our hearts. We fought to obey commands that only reminded us of our failures. But everything has changed! God has done what the law never could—He's given us new hearts, filled with His Spirit."

He continued, his gaze unwavering. "We're not just following a list of dos and don'ts anymore—we're being led from within! The Spirit Himself has come to dwell in us, transforming our desires. Walking by the Spirit means more than just obeying external commands; it's living in a freedom that starts from the inside and works its way out. It's a life where the Spirit Himself shapes our choices, our actions, our very nature."

Paul's voice softened but remained intense, his words brimming with life.

"It's not about striving to be good anymore—it's about being made new. It's about living by the Spirit's power, discovering that His voice within us leads to true victory, moment by moment, day by day. It's no longer a burden we carry—it's a new life that carries us."

Paul leaned forward. "When you walk by the Spirit, you're no longer bound by the law of sin and death.[1] The desires of the flesh still whisper, still tempt, but they no longer rule us. God has broken sin's power over us.[2] He gives us His strength to resist the flesh and the power to live in a way that truly honors God."

CHAPTER 29

THE FRUIT OF THE SPIRIT

(GALATIANS 5:19–26)

TERTIUS SAT BACK, resting the reed pen in the inkwell, a satisfied smile crossing his tired face. Paul's words were like light and life—a sharp contrast to the rigid, academic instruction he was accustomed to.

"It's beautiful, sir," he said wistfully. "I've never seen it so clearly. And I've never felt it so deeply."

"Good!" Paul exclaimed, his eyes brightening. "That makes me very happy. I hope that everyone who reads it will feel the same way."

"I think they will, sir." Tertius rubbed his eyes with the back of his hands, the long hours of work finally catching up to him. "I think there's something very special about this letter. I wouldn't be surprised if it's copied and distributed far beyond Galatia."

Paul gave a wide yawn, the kind that made Tertius yawn in response. Catching him in the act, Paul chuckled.

"Well, Tertius," he said, "whoever reads this letter, I just pray God floods their hearts with the light of the glorious gospel."

He glanced toward the window. The last traces of daylight were fading into twilight. "By the way, it's getting late. Are you all right to keep working?"

Tertius stretched, stifling another yawn. "Yes, sir, but I might need some light myself to continue."

Paul nodded, glancing around the dim room. "Yes, light would be good."

Paul crossed the room to the triangular shelf tucked into the corner, where lamps, wicks, and squat jars of oil stood in careful rows. He picked up a worn clay lamp and carefully poured oil into the reservoir. After watching it settle, he twisted a wick and threaded it through the spout.

He carried it over to Tertius, who had already crossed to the fireplace, where the small brazier rested among the soot-blackened stones. Paul extended the lamp. Tertius picked up the tongs that lay beside the brazier and lifted a glowing coal from the embers. Holding it close, he let the heat lick at the wick until it smoldered, then gave a soft breath. The flame flared, caught, and a steady glow rose.

Paul placed the lamp on the writing table next to the letter, its warm light spilling over the parchment. "There. That should help," he said, with a tired but contented smile, as he eased into his chair across from Tertius.

Tertius blinked against the new light as his eyes adjusted. "Thank you, sir," he said, picking up his reed pen again.

Paul reached for the basket of fruit on the table beside him, his fingers brushing over the figs, grapes, and dates. He selected a fig and bit into it slowly, savoring the sweetness while gazing thoughtfully at the jar. After taking another bite, Paul nudged the basket toward Tertius. "Go on, have something. We've earned it."

Tertius smiled and reached for a date, rolling it between his fingers before eating it. Paul leaned back in his chair as the room settled into a comfortable silence, broken only by the sounds of their quiet chewing.

As Paul ate the last morsel of his fig, he turned the remaining stem between his fingers, eyes thoughtful. "You know, this fruit doesn't grow because the branches strain or strive. It grows naturally, effortlessly—as long as it stays connected to the vine."

Tertius looked up, searching for the meaning behind Paul's words.

"Jesus said, 'By their fruit, you will know them,'" Paul continued, wiping his hands on his tunic. "In other words, you can recognize a tree by the fruit it bears. But it works the other way around too, doesn't it? You can tell what kind of fruit a tree will produce just by knowing what kind of tree it is. A fig tree will always yield figs—not dates or olives. It's the same with us. The source of our life determines the fruit we bear. The Spirit will always produce spiritual fruit. The flesh will always produce fleshly fruit. It's inevitable."

Tertius nodded, his mind already turning to the implications of Paul's words.

Paul leaned forward. "Write this: **'When you follow the desires of your [flesh], the results are very clear: sexual immorality, impurity, lustful pleasures, idolatry, sorcery, hostility, quarreling, jealousy, outbursts of anger, selfish ambition, dissension, division, envy, drunkenness, wild parties, and other sins like these. Let me tell you again, as I have before, that anyone living that sort of life will not inherit the Kingdom of God'**" (5:19–21).

Tertius scratched the words onto the parchment.

"But," Paul said, "the fruit of the *Spirit*...now that's something different entirely. It's not born of effort or striving. It's the natural outflow of being connected to God through the Holy Spirit."

He paused, his eyes reflecting the importance of his next words. "Write this: **'But the Holy Spirit produces this kind of fruit in our lives: love, joy, peace, patience, kindness, goodness, faithfulness, gentleness, and self-control. There is no law against these things!'**" (5:22–23)

Paul's voice softened, almost as though he were musing aloud as he continued dictating. **"Those who belong to Christ Jesus have nailed the passions and desires of their [flesh] to his cross**

and crucified them there. Since we are living by the Spirit, let us follow the Spirit's leading in every part of our lives. Let us not become conceited, or provoke one another, or be jealous of one another" (5:24–26).

Tertius etched the final words into the parchment. The room grew still once more, the glow of the lamp casting flickering shadows on the walls.

"Sir, can you help me understand how this all ties together? We've talked about walking in the Spirit, but now you're speaking of crucifying the passions and desires of the flesh. Are these two separate ideas? And how do we 'crucify' ourselves?"

Paul looked up, his expression pensive, carefully weighing the best way to respond.

"They're not separate at all, Tertius. In fact, they are intimately connected. Walking in the Spirit and crucifying the passions of the flesh are two sides of the same coin."

Tertius nodded, though his expression remained clouded.

"Think of it this way," Paul said. "When we walk by the Spirit, we make a choice—a choice to follow His leading. Saying yes to the Spirit means saying no to the desires of the flesh. And that, Tertius, is where crucifixion comes in.

"When we put our faith in Jesus, we trusted His work on the cross to save us. In baptism, we identified with His death and resurrection. Our old self—ruled by selfishness and sin—was crucified with Him. It lost its authority. We stepped into a new life, under a new ruler. The flesh no longer commands us. Now we follow the Spirit."[1]

Paul pressed on.

"That's exactly what Jesus meant when He told His disciples to take up their cross and follow Him. Following Jesus means dying to the things that pull us away from God. And the truth is, we already are dead to them. The problem isn't that the flesh still has power—it's that we forget it doesn't.[2] The Spirit renews our minds, teaching us to recognize that the old voice—the voice of self—is no longer in charge. We now have the mind of Christ,[3] united with the Spirit, giving us access to the very thoughts of God. And the more we listen, the clearer His voice becomes."

Paul's voice lowered as he spoke with a gentle understanding. "So, you see, Tertius, walking in the Spirit and crucifying the flesh aren't two separate tasks—they're one and the same. To follow the Spirit is to leave the flesh behind. And when we do, we bear His fruit—not by striving, but simply by staying connected to the vine."

CHAPTER 30

RESTORING THE FALLEN

(GALATIANS 6:1–3)

TERTIUS RUBBED HIS temples, clearly grappling with something unspoken.

Paul, glancing up, immediately sensed the tension: doubt—not of the gospel itself, but of its implications.

"Come on, Tertius. I know that look. Out with it."

Tertius hesitated, looking down at his parchment. "Sir, I understand everything you've been saying about walking in the Spirit, crucifying the flesh...but I can't help but wonder...what about the reality of sin?"

Paul raised an eyebrow, signaling him to continue.

"I mean, you admit that even you still struggle against the flesh. If that's the case for someone as spiritually mature as you, then what hope is there for the rest of us? I understand that we're supposed to walk in the Spirit and crucify the flesh, but what happens if we fail, if people in the church fall short? How do we hold them accountable? The law had its answers, but what do we have now?"

Tertius stopped abruptly, realizing how much he had let spill out. The room fell silent, and for a moment he wondered if he'd crossed a line. But then Paul smiled—a warm, knowing smile, as though he had been waiting for this very moment.

"Write this," Paul began, without a preface. **"Dear brothers**

and sisters, if another believer is overcome by some sin, you who are godly should gently and humbly help that person back onto the right path. And be careful not to fall into the same temptation yourself. Share each other's burdens, and in this way obey the law of Christ" (6:1–2).

As Tertius wrote the words, he was struck by their power. They were so simple yet so profound.

Paul stood and began pacing slowly as he elaborated. "Under the law, the only response to failure is judgment. But the gospel offers something different: grace. When we walk by the Spirit, our first instinct isn't to condemn or shame—it's to restore, just as Jesus did for us. When you truly understand the depth of God's grace and mercy through Jesus, you can't help but offer that same grace and mercy to others. That's why I said we should 'gently and humbly help that person,' because we've all been in need of that same grace."

Tertius hesitated, doubt still evident in his voice. "But isn't there a risk that we'll end up tolerating sin? That if we're too lenient, people will just continue to fall?"

"That's the fear, isn't it?" Paul said. "That grace might be too soft, too permissive. But grace isn't about ignoring sin. It's about responding to it with the Spirit's power. And don't mistake gentleness for weakness. Restoring someone takes more strength, more courage, more spiritual maturity than simply handing out judgment."

Tertius nodded, taking in Paul's words.

"We all need grace, Tertius. None of us are beyond stumbling. That's why I said, 'Be careful not to fall into the same temptation yourself.' If you think you're too morally superior to fall, you're setting yourself up for it. Even as we restore others, we must stay humble and vigilant, or we might fall too."

Paul continued. "The law of Christ is to love one another. And love means we don't just watch others fall—we bear their burdens. We don't distance ourselves from the weak; we share in their struggles. That's true strength. That's what Jesus modeled for us, and it's part of what it looks like to live by the Spirit."

Tertius was awestruck. Paul had used an impossible question to reveal a deeper truth—one where grace didn't mean a free pass to sin but an opportunity for redemption.

Paul stood at the window, hands clasped behind his back. He drew a deep breath, then said, "Write this as well: **'If you think you are too important to help someone, you are only fooling yourself. You are not that important'**" (6:3).[1]

Tertius chuckled softly, the seriousness of the subject lightened momentarily by Paul's bluntness. But Paul's gaze remained intense, his expression thoughtful. Tertius finished writing and waited for Paul to elaborate.

"Have you ever heard the parable Jesus told about the Good Samaritan, Tertius?" Paul asked suddenly, turning to face him.

Tertius blinked, caught off guard. "No, sir. I'm not familiar with it."

Paul nodded slowly, as if recalling the moment he first heard the story himself.

Tertius set his pen down, his attention fully on Paul.

"There was a man," Paul began, "a Jew, traveling from Jerusalem to Jericho. Along the way, robbers attacked him. They stripped him, beat him, and left him half-dead by the road. Now, by chance, a priest came down that same road. A priest, Tertius—someone who knew the law, who believed he understood righteousness. But when he saw the wounded man, he passed by on the other side, refusing to help. Then came a Levite, another man of the law, a servant of God. But like the priest, when he saw the beaten man, he too crossed over and passed by.

"But then," Paul continued, "a Samaritan came along. You know how Jews view Samaritans—outcasts, despised. Yet when this Samaritan saw the man, something different happened. He didn't react with disdain or judgment. He was moved with compassion. He went to the man, bandaged his wounds, poured oil and wine on them to cleanse and soothe. He lifted the man onto his own donkey and took him to an inn, where he cared for him."

Paul's voice softened. "When Jesus told this story, He asked a question: 'Which of these three was a neighbor to the man who was attacked?' Obviously the one who showed mercy, right?"

Tertius nodded in agreement quietly.

Paul locked his earnest eyes on Tertius as he continued. "Do you see it, Tertius? The priest and the Levite—men of the law—they crossed the road to avoid helping the fallen. That's what religious pride does. It looks at the broken, those who've stumbled, with disgust and walks by. It's too self-important to take the time to restore someone who's fallen. It's the same with the Judaizers. They boast in their obedience, proud of how clean they've kept their hands—but they won't lift a finger to help someone who's fallen. When it comes to real compassion—real love—they completely miss it."

Paul's eyes gleamed with passion. "But the Good Samaritan—that's the heart of Jesus. The one who stops. The one who doesn't care about reputation or status. The one who isn't worried about getting his religious garments dirty. He stoops down, binds up wounds, carries the broken. That's the difference between religious pride and the gospel of grace. The gospel doesn't leave us beaten by sin on the side of the road. It lifts us up. It heals. It restores."

CHAPTER 31

YOU REAP WHAT YOU SOW

(GALATIANS 6:4–5)

PAUL GLANCED AT the nearly completed jar, the dim lamplight casting soft, waving shadows across its fractured yet beautifully restored surface. Only one shard remained.

He moved to the corner shelf and retrieved another lamp. With steady hands, he poured oil from a small clay jug, watching it settle before trimming a fresh wick. He set it inside and lit it from the flame already burning on the writing table.

Paul returned to the table beneath the window, his gaze falling on the final shard. The last piece. The one that would complete the restoration—and drive home the heart of his message to the Galatians. He picked it up, turning it in his hands, running his thumb over the etched words. This was it. The culmination of everything.

Tertius sat quietly, pen in hand, watching.

Paul studied the smaller writing on the shard for a long moment, then read the heading aloud: **"You Reap What You Sow."** His voice was quiet, almost solemn, as if the phrase would be carried beyond the room. He carefully applied resin to the jagged edges and pressed the final shard into place. A soft click sounded as the piece settled snugly, completing the jar.

"There," Paul murmured, stepping back to admire the now-restored vessel. "It's finished."

Tertius blinked, his gaze fixed on the jar glimmering in the lamplight—a visible metaphor for the journey through Paul's letter. But his mind lingered on the words just spoken: "You reap what you sow."

Without waiting for the question Tertius hadn't yet asked, Paul spoke again, his voice steady and clear. The words flowed, as if the message had been waiting all along for this final moment.

"Write this," Paul said, his eyes still on the jar. **"Pay careful attention to your own work, for then you will get the satisfaction of a job well done, and you won't need to compare yourself to anyone else. For we are each responsible for our own conduct"** (6:4–5).

As Tertius finished writing, his gaze lingered on the parchment, a puzzled look on his face. "But sir, isn't the whole message of the gospel that our righteousness comes from Christ's work, not our own? Now it almost sounds like you're telling us to take pride in our actions. How can that be? Doesn't that contradict what you've been teaching?"

Paul smiled, reading the hesitation in Tertius' face. He leaned forward, resting his hands on the writing table. "I'm glad you're wrestling with this, Tertius. It means you're listening. And you're right—our righteousness comes from Christ alone. We can't earn it. We don't climb some ladder to reach God. He came down to us. That's grace. That's the gospel. But what I'm saying now isn't a contradiction. Let me explain."

Tertius nodded, ready for clarity.

"When I talk about testing your actions or taking responsibility for your conduct, I'm not saying you can earn righteousness before God. That's impossible. We're not saved *by* good works. But we are saved *for* good works. There's a difference. We're not working *for* salvation, but we are working *out* our salvation. This is about living in the freedom Christ has given us and making sure we use that freedom well."

Paul's face grew serious. "The Judaizers' problem isn't just bad theology—it's pride. People who try to prove themselves by works end up in constant competition. They measure their value against others, boasting in their influence and tearing down anyone who threatens their status. That's what they're doing with the Galatians—and with me. So when I say, 'Pay attention to your own work, and you won't need to compare yourself to anyone else,' it's a rebuke. But it's also a warning: Comparison is a trap. Focusing on others is often a way of avoiding the real issue—our own hearts."

Paul exhaled deeply. "I know this trap well. As Pharisees, we prided ourselves on righteousness, but holiness wasn't about God—it was a contest. We made sure everyone saw us. We prayed in the synagogues and on the street corners, robed in dignity, voices lifted—not to reach heaven, but to impress anyone within earshot."

Then, with a dramatic flourish, Paul lifted both hands high, palms open to the heavens. Tilting his head back, he raised his voice, rich with mock piety: "God, I thank You that I am not like other sinners! I fast twice a week. I tithe on everything. I keep the law. What a righteous man I am."

Then, just as abruptly, Paul lowered his arms, shaking his head with disgust. His voice softened. "It was never about true devotion, Tertius. It was a performance. A way to be seen, admired."

His gaze met Tertius'. "But righteousness isn't measured by how you stack up against others. You can always find someone who looks worse than you. But that comparison doesn't make you holy—it just feeds your pride."

Paul tapped the table. "That's why I say, 'We are each responsible for our own conduct.' When we stand before God, He won't compare us to others. He'll look at our own faithfulness."

Tertius set his reed pen down for a moment, his expression more relaxed as things began to fall into place. Then a fresh question surfaced.

"Sir," he began cautiously, "you just said we should bear one another's burdens to fulfill the law of Christ. But now you're saying each should carry their own load. Isn't *that* a contradiction?"

Paul smiled warmly. "No, Tertius. That's not a contradiction either. Let me explain. When I talk about bearing one another's burdens, I'm referring to the struggles and hardships we face—our failures, weaknesses, and sins. We're called to support each other, to lift each other up when we fall. That's the law of Christ—the law of love. We don't let our brothers and sisters struggle alone."

Paul let the words linger before continuing. "But when I say each should carry their own load, I'm talking about personal responsibility. No one can live your life for you. No one else can make your decisions or stand in your place on the day of judgment. We'll each be held accountable for our own choices, our own faithfulness. That's not something we can pass on to others."

Tertius, processing, glanced at the jar. His eyes lingered on the final shard Paul had placed, seamlessly joining the rest of the vessel.

"Sir," Tertius ventured, "what does this all have to do with the last note you wrote on that shard? 'You reap what you sow'?"

Paul nodded, pleased with Tertius' attentiveness. He folded his hands, drawing all the threads together. "Ah, Tertius, that's the heart of it. The principle of reaping and sowing—it's as old as creation itself. It's woven into the very fabric of the universe, both in the physical and spiritual sense. Whether we're talking about planting seeds in the ground or the choices we make in life, the principle is the same: What you plant is what you'll harvest."

Tertius nodded, though Paul sensed he was still looking for more.

Paul's voice took on a quiet urgency. "It goes back to our earlier conversation. The flesh is mortal. It is subject to corruption.[1] Therefore, when we sow to the flesh, we reap corruption. But the Spirit produces good fruit in our lives. When we bear each other's burdens, when we restore someone with gentleness, we're sowing seeds of love, grace, and compassion—seeds that will bear fruit in others and in our own souls. And when we take responsibility for our own actions, when we carry our own load, we're sowing seeds of integrity and faithfulness—seeds that will yield a reward, not just in this life, but in eternity."

CHAPTER 32

SEEDS AND SCARS

(GALATIANS 6:6)

PAUL SAT BACK in his chair, admiring his work. The jar stood tall, its amphora shape carefully restored after being shattered into seven pieces, each crack sealed with resin. The seams of its reconstruction remained visible, giving the jar character—once fractures, now stories. From one angle they looked like scars; from another, they traced like roads across a reddish-brown terra-cotta map.

The two looped handles, practical yet graceful, stood firm. Around the ornate neck and body, a faded motif of wildflowers—delicate yellow blooms and green stems—stretched like whispers from a forgotten season, worn by time and weathered by Paul's journeys.

Though it bore the marks of its past, the jar had become something more—beautiful not only in spite of its brokenness but because of it, standing as a testament to the care and patience that had made it whole again.

Tertius, still gazing at the jar with Paul, found himself more curious than ever. Paul had promised to share the story behind it, but the day was nearly over and the jar's restoration was complete. Where had it come from? Why was Paul so captivated by it? Why had he chosen today to work on it? And why had he written notes to himself on the inner surface of its fragments?

Breaking the silence, Tertius spoke up. "Well, sir, it looks like all your fragments have been used. All your notes are inside. Now what?"

Paul looked at him with a tired smile. "We're not done with the last note yet, my friend. Do you remember what it was?"

"You reap what you sow," Tertius responded, dipping his reed pen into the ink, ready for the next dictation.

Paul nodded. "Write this: **'Those who are taught the word of God should provide for their teachers, sharing all good things with them'**" (6:6).[1] He watched as Tertius carefully recorded the words.

After a pause, Tertius couldn't hold back any longer. "I don't mean to overstep, sir, but you've been working on this jar all day. I can't contain my curiosity anymore."

A smile danced on Paul's lips. "All right, Tertius. You've been patient enough. Let me tell you the story."

Tertius set his reed pen down with quiet eagerness, his eyes fixed on Paul.

Paul shifted in his chair, turning slightly to face the small table by the window. He gestured with his left hand toward the jar resting there.

"This jar," Paul began, "was a gift from the Galatians."

"From the Galatians?"

Paul's eyes softened, his voice carrying the weight of both warmth and sorrow.

"Yes," he said, nodding slowly. "They gave it to me on one of my earlier visits. They pooled their resources to purchase it. And inside, they tucked letters—words of encouragement, simple notes of gratitude, reminders of the bond we shared. It wasn't just a gift, Tertius. It was their hearts poured out in clay. A symbol of faith. A token of love. A reminder that once, their passion for the gospel burned as brightly as their love for me.

"Back then, it felt like a glimpse of heaven on earth. In fact," Paul continued, "it's their generosity that came to mind when I dictated the very line we just wrote: **'Those who are taught the word of God should provide for their teachers, sharing all good things with them.'** The Galatians understood that principle well.

"I still remember how they cared for me tenderly when I was weak and in need. They didn't turn away or shrink back. They welcomed me as though I were an angel from God—no, as though I were Christ Jesus Himself."

Paul's eyes lit up at the memory. "Remember I told you there was a time when they would have given me their very eyes if it had been possible. That's how deep their love ran. They sowed into my ministry with more than just words—they gave generously, even when they didn't have much to give. And those seeds, Tertius, were seeds of love and faith.

"This is why I'm reminding them that those who receive from the Word should give back to those who teach it. It's not about duty—it's about love. After all, we've been talking about sowing and reaping, haven't we? I want them to recall who they once were—how God poured out His blessings on them in those early days. Their generosity wasn't just a habit then; it was a sign of the Spirit's work in their hearts. But now that joy of giving seems to have faded, and I believe it's the influence of those who led them astray.

"Remember, we discussed the difference between the works of the flesh and the fruit of the Spirit: Our fruit reflects our roots. When we're grounded in grace, generosity flows naturally. But when tangled in rules and fear, we harvest selfishness and scarcity."

Tertius nodded, but his gaze lingered on the jar, curiosity still clear. "But the jar, sir...how did it break?"

Paul sighed. "During one of my journeys, I was attacked by a mob. In the chaos, this jar was shattered—just as I nearly was." His eyes darkened briefly, the memory of the brutal attack flashing through his mind.

Tertius' face grew serious. He knew of Paul's many persecutions, but this jar—this seemingly insignificant object—now carried far more meaning.

"I couldn't bear to throw the pieces away," Paul said. "I had planned to restore it, but when I heard how the Galatians had been led astray by the Judaizers, I couldn't even look at the shards anymore. What had once been a token of love became a painful reminder of the brokenness in their faith. So I put them away. Out of sight, out of mind."

Paul continued. "I had sowed seeds of the gospel among the Galatians and reaped a harvest of salvation. They had sowed seeds of love into me and reaped many blessings. But then...the Judaizers came. They sowed seeds of doubt, of righteousness based on works. And now the Galatians are reaping confusion, division, and the loss of the freedom they once had in Christ."

Paul let the silence hang for a moment. "Months later, when I began thinking about writing this letter, I found myself looking for shards of pottery to make notes on for myself, as I often do when parchment isn't needed."

Tertius nodded, familiar with the practice of using broken pottery for everyday writing.

"That's when I found the pieces," Paul went on. "The broken fragments of the Galatian jar. And that's when it hit me, Tertius. It felt fitting—almost poetic—to write my notes on these very shards. As I held each piece, remembering what it had been, the message I needed to send began to take shape. I saw the parallel. Restoring this jar would be a visible symbol of what I hoped to accomplish by writing this letter—the restoration of their faith, of our friendship, and of their broken community as a whole."

Tertius sat back, eyes wide with understanding as Paul's words took on new meaning.

"That's why we're writing this letter," Paul said softly. "To remind them of who they once were, to help them see the truth that brought such blessing into their lives. I want them to know the broken pieces can be put back together—that something beautiful can come from this mess."[2]

Tertius looked at the jar with new eyes. It was far more meaningful than he had realized. "What will you do with it now, sir?"

A mischievous glint appeared in Paul's eyes as a slow smile spread across his face. "You'll see."

Tertius laughed, shaking his head. "You always have another surprise up your sleeve, don't you?"

Paul chuckled, leaning back in his chair. "Well, the sooner we finish this letter, the sooner you'll find out."

CHAPTER 33

GROWING WEARY

(GALATIANS 6:7–10)

A SOFT KNOCK ECHOED through the small room. Paul and Tertius paused, their conversation momentarily interrupted. The knock came again, polite but firm.

Tertius crossed the room to open the door, revealing the young servant holding a lamp aloft, its warm glow casting animated shadows across his face.

"Good evening," the boy said respectfully. "My master invites you both to join him for dinner. It's nearly ready."

Paul smiled, nodding. "Thank you. Please tell Gaius we will join him shortly."

The servant bowed slightly and disappeared into the night, the light from his lamp fading as he went.

Tertius closed the door and returned to his seat. "Dinner already? The day has gone quickly, hasn't it?"

Paul rubbed his tired eyes. "It has. But before we go, we should finish the thought that was written on that last shard."

"You reap what you sow," Tertius said with a smile. He dipped his reed pen into the ink, ready for the next dictation.

Paul spoke slowly. "Write this: **'Don't be misled—you cannot mock the justice of God. You will always harvest what you plant. Those who live only to satisfy their own [flesh] will harvest**

decay and death from that [flesh]. But those who live to please the Spirit will harvest everlasting life from the Spirit'" (6:7–8).[1]

Paul waited for Tertius to finish his transcription. But after finishing the last line, Tertius hesitated.

"Sir, it seems like this theme of sowing and reaping has really shifted the tone of the letter. In the beginning we were refuting the idea of a works-based righteousness. You were quite passionate about that."

Paul crossed his arms, nodding in agreement as he waited for the rest of the thought.

"But now," Tertius continued, "you seem to be emphasizing the importance of works—of personal responsibility and consequences for our actions."

Paul leaned back, a thoughtful smile on his face. "Yes, Tertius, I've said it before, and I'll say it again—you are not saved *by* good works, but you are saved *for* good works. The truth remains, and I hope no one reading this letter will ever miss it. You always reap what you sow. To deny that would be utter folly."

"But sir," Tertius said, "I thought the Galatians *did* sow good seeds. They received you and the gospel with joy. They welcomed the message, turned from idols, and began living by faith. It seemed like everything was moving in the right direction. So what happened? Why did they lose heart?"

Paul sighed and looked out the window. "Well, Tertius, the process of sowing and reaping doesn't happen overnight, does it? The fruit we eat in one season was planted in the last. And that waiting period…it's where many falter. That's where discouragement slips in and makes them vulnerable."

He continued. "The Galatians, they started strong. They planted good seeds, walking in faith, reaping the blessings of salvation. In the beginning it was all so fresh and exciting. They were filled with joy, as if Jesus might return at any moment. They had that first love fire."

Paul's voice took on a more contemplative tone. "But over

time they began to grow weary. The excitement faded, and with it, their expectations. They had hoped for quicker results, an easier path with fewer struggles. But the reality of life didn't align with their hopes. They faced persecution, hardships, and their own internal battles. And when things didn't go the way they'd hoped, they started to wonder if something was wrong."

Tertius looked at Paul with solemn, weary eyes, relating deeply to the notion of growing tired.

"You see, Tertius, when you don't see immediate results from your faith, it's easy to grow weary. It's easy to lose heart when the harvest seems far off. And that's when the enemy strikes!"

Tertius nodded slowly, understanding dawning on his face.

"The Judaizers sowed seeds of doubt, convincing them that something was missing in their faith. They told the Galatians that the answer wasn't deeper trust—but works: circumcision, rituals, the works of the law."

Paul stood and began pacing, his voice rising with intensity. "Isn't that always the temptation when things don't go as we plan? We start to doubt the method and think, 'Maybe I need to do something new, something different, to force the results.' And that's when we become susceptible to the temptation to get impatient."

Realization dawned on Tertius' face. "It's the same mistake Abraham made, isn't it, sir?"

"Go on," Paul said, encouraging Tertius to expand on the thought.

"Well, instead of trusting that God would fulfill His promise in His time, Abraham and Sarah took matters into their own hands. And that's how Ishmael was born."

"Right!" Paul responded. "That's what happens when you get impatient."

His voice softened as he continued. "Write this down: **'So let's not get tired of doing what is good. At just the right time we will reap a harvest of blessing if we don't give up'**" (6:9).

Tertius smiled as he finished the sentence. "This is good, sir. Are we finished with the sowing and reaping theme now?"

Paul returned the smile but shook his head gently. "There's one more thing, Tertius. The false teaching in Galatia has caused people to turn inward—navel-gazing, fixated on whether they're doing enough. They're focused on themselves, anxious and divided, obsessed with their own standing."

Tertius shook his head in dismay.

Paul continued. "I don't want them to hear this sowing and reaping talk as yet another invitation to selfishness. Instead of fixating on themselves, they need to focus on sowing seeds of goodness, love, and generosity into the lives of their brothers and sisters in Christ. That's where true freedom lies—when you stop focusing on yourself and start living for God and others.

"Write this down, Tertius: **'Therefore, whenever we have the opportunity, we should do good to everyone—especially to those in the family of faith'**" (6:10).

Tertius carefully penned the words. The only sounds in the room were his reed pen gliding across the parchment and soft crackling from the oil lamp.

A knock interrupted the quiet. The servant reappeared at the door.

"Dinner is ready, sirs," he said.

Paul smiled and stretched his stiff limbs. "Let's not keep our host waiting."

CHAPTER 34

THE EVENING MEAL

THE EVENING AIR was crisp as Paul and Tertius followed the young servant, his oil lamp casting a soft glow along the stone path. The well-tended garden stretched out before them, bathed in the twilight, with the last streaks of daylight fading into the horizon. The leaves rustled softly, and the distant sound of a nightingale's song mingled with the murmur of voices carried on the wind.

As they passed through a narrow archway, the faint scent of roasted lamb and freshly baked bread filled the air, teasing their senses with the promise of a warm meal.

Paul glanced at Tertius, a faint smile teasing the corners of his mouth. "It's been a long day, hasn't it?"

Tertius nodded, his attention drawn ahead as they stepped inside the house.

The dining area, though simple, had an elegance to it. The walls were adorned with tapestries and frescoes and flickering shadows cast by the oil lamps. A low, cushioned triclinium was arranged around the dining table, where guests would recline to eat, propped on their left elbows as was the custom in Roman-style dining.

At the head of the table, Gaius—tall and broad-shouldered—stood near a bronze brazier that provided warmth against the cool night air. His graying beard framed a face that exuded both strength and kindness.

"Welcome, my friends!" Gaius called out. He stretched his

arms wide in greeting, his deep red tunic catching the lamplight. "You're just in time."

Paul nodded appreciatively. "Thank you, my friend. It was thoughtful of you to invite us to dinner."

Gaius smiled, his eyes crinkling at the corners. "The honor is mine, Paul. Please, recline. You've earned a good meal."

The air was rich with the mouthwatering aromas of roasted lamb, bread, and herbs. Platters of olives, figs, and cheeses adorned the table, along with bowls of lentils and dates. A large krater stood nearby, where wine had already been mixed with water, ready to be poured into each guest's cup.

At the center of the feast sat a large dish of lamb, perfectly seasoned, its juices glistening in the soft light. A servant moved gracefully between the guests, setting down freshly baked flatbreads and pouring wine into each cup.

Tertius adjusted himself on the couch, settling into the reclining posture. His eyes lingered on the table's bounty, but a brief hesitation crossed his face—this was the first time he had ever dined in a Gentile's home. But Paul's earlier words echoed in his mind: "There is neither Jew nor Gentile...for you are all one in Christ Jesus." A sense of calm washed over him. This was the freedom Paul had spoken of—the unity that transcended old boundaries.

The servant finished his task, stepping back into the shadows and leaving them to enjoy the meal in peace.

As the savory smells of the feast filled the room, Tertius found his mind still turning over the events of the day, the depth of their conversation utterly stimulating despite the physical toll.

Paul took a piece of bread and dipped it into the olive oil, letting out a slow breath as he rested his weight more comfortably against the cushions. Across from him, Gaius reached for his own portion, his movements relaxed yet observant.

"It's nearly finished then?" Gaius asked as he took a bite.

Paul nodded, setting down his cup. "Yes, we're close. Just a few final words left to write."

Gaius smiled, a knowing look in his eyes as he turned his gaze to Tertius. "It's been quite the journey, hasn't it?"

"Yes, it has, sir. It feels...significant," the scribe said, nodding in agreement.

"Well done, both of you," Gaius said with the warmth of a father encouraging his children. "Paul, I'm sure you've poured your heart into it."

"I have," Paul replied. "There was a special grace with us today, even amidst the rebukes and stern warnings against the Judaizers."

Gaius raised an eyebrow. "So you went after them, eh? Hearing how fired up you were last night, I thought they might be in for it."

Paul shook his head firmly. "I couldn't hold back. There's too much at stake. These men...they aren't just teaching false doctrine. They're preaching a different gospel entirely—one that threatens the very future of the church."

Gaius nodded slowly, taking in Paul's words. Then he turned to Tertius, making sure he felt included in the conversation. "Why do you think they're so intent on dragging the Galatians back under the law?"

"It's about power," Tertius replied boldly. He glanced at Paul, who gave him an approving look. "They want control over the Galatians."

"That's right," Paul said, his eyes lighting up. "They want the Galatians to focus on their own efforts—circumcision, rituals, the works of the law—so they stop looking to Christ and start depending on these false teachers and their rules."

"And yet wasn't it Christ Himself who set us free from that very burden?" Gaius added.

"Yes!" Tertius said, leaning forward, his words gaining momentum. "And it's not just freedom from the law; it's the freedom to live by the Spirit! The entire message, from start to finish, has been about the true gospel—how Christ has redeemed us from the curse of the law by becoming a curse for us. We're justified by faith in Christ alone, not by our own works or circumcision. We are children of the promise, heirs through faith, not slaves bound to rules and rituals. And those who try to justify themselves through the law have severed themselves from grace."

Paul and Gaius exchanged glances, both taken aback by the fire in Tertius' voice. Paul settled back once more, a proud smile spreading across his face, while Gaius watched Tertius with new-found admiration.

Tertius paused, catching his breath. Then he pressed on, the truth he had been scribing all day now surging within him.

"Paul rebuked the Galatians for turning away to a different gospel, for letting themselves be ensnared by false teachers. The law served its purpose as a guardian, yes, but now that Christ has come, we're no longer under its yoke. We've been crucified with Christ; it's no longer we who live, but Christ who lives in us! This freedom doesn't mean living recklessly—it means walking in step with the Spirit, sowing to the Spirit, and serving one another in love. It's about returning to the simplicity of the gospel—Christ and Him crucified."

Paul smiled, meeting Tertius' gaze. "Well said, Tertius. You've got it. The Holy Spirit has made the message real to you."

Gaius, who had been watching in quiet awe, broke his silence. "Remarkable," he said, his deep voice filled with respect. "Tertius, you've not only learned the message but embraced it with your whole heart. That is rare and precious."

Turning his gaze to Paul, Gaius said, "You've done more than just write a letter, Paul. You've passed the gospel's power on to others. If the Galatians receive this letter with even half the passion Tertius has shown tonight, it will bear much fruit."

Gaius lifted his cup toward Tertius. "May you carry this truth with you always, my friend. What you've found is more than knowledge—it's life itself."

The conversation lightened after that, the room filling with the warmth of laughter and stories shared between friends. They spoke of their travels, the people they had met, and the work still ahead. The scent of roasted lamb and herbs lingered in the air, and the crackling of the fire added a comforting backdrop to their conversation. It was a moment of shared peace, the joy of breaking bread together after a long day's labor.

As the meal drew to a close, Gaius set his cup down and cast a glance at Paul. Normally, fellowship like this would stretch late into the evening. But tonight Gaius could sense Paul's restlessness. His fingers tapped lightly on the table, his eyes twinkling with a quiet urgency, as though his mind was already racing ahead to the unfinished parchment waiting for him.

With a knowing smile, Gaius asked, "Is there anything else I can do for you, Paul?"

Paul looked up, gratitude in his eyes. "Yes, actually. Could you have the courier ready to leave at first light? The letter will be finished by morning."

Gaius blinked. "Tomorrow morning? I didn't realize you were that close."

Paul nodded. "Yes, we've made good progress. There's still a bit more to say, but we'll finish tonight. This letter needs to reach Galatia as soon as possible."

"Very well," Gaius said. "I'll make sure the courier is ready. He is lodging very close to here. I'll have him waiting." He raised his cup one last time. "To the safe delivery of your words, Paul. And to the restoration of those who need them."

Paul stood, stretching his tired limbs. "Thank you, my friend. You've been more than generous."

As Gaius clasped Paul's shoulder in a gesture of friendship, he watched the two men step out into the cool night air, their task nearly complete.

CHAPTER 35

BIG LETTERS

(GALATIANS 6:11–18)

ABOVE THEM, THE sky stretched out in a blanket of stars as Paul and Tertius made their way back to the guest room. A breeze rustled through the nearby olive trees, filling the silence between them as they walked. Neither man spoke, their minds occupied with the burden of the unfinished task ahead.

As they entered the small familiar space, Tertius moved quickly to the table and rearranged the parchment, ink, and reed pen, preparing for the final dictation. They were close to finishing—just one final section remained, the closing words to seal the message they had painstakingly written together.

Paul didn't speak. He sat still, his eyes locked on the parchment, a contemplative silence hanging in the air. Tertius waited, sensing that something had shifted in Paul's mind. And then, without warning, Paul's expression changed. A quiet determination settled over him.

"Get up, Tertius," Paul said, his voice steady but resolute.

Tertius blinked, taken aback. "Sir?"

Paul looked at him, a faint but unmistakable smile forming. "Get up," he repeated. "I need to write this part myself."

Tertius hesitated for a moment, surprised by the unexpected

instruction. But he obeyed without question, rising from his seat and stepping aside.

It was a rare sight—Paul, who had dictated every word up until now, taking the reed pen into his own hand. He dipped it into the ink, his eyes intense with focus.

Tertius stood back, watching in silence. He had nearly forgotten, in all these hours of listening and scribing, just who Paul truly was. Paul wasn't merely a teacher or preacher—he was a scholar of unparalleled wisdom, an apostle, a man whose words carried the power to shape the future of the church and the world. And now, as Paul sat down to write the final lines himself, it was as though a master craftsman had picked up his own tools, deciding to complete the work with his own hands.

Paul began to write. Tertius stood behind him, reading along silently as the words took shape: **"NOTICE WHAT LARGE LETTERS I USE AS I WRITE THESE CLOSING WORDS IN MY OWN HANDWRITING"** (6:11).

Paul set the reed pen down and looked at the bold strokes he'd just scrawled, a crooked smile forming on his lips. "It's…it's been a while since I've done this," he muttered, eyes narrowing as he tilted the parchment to inspect the uneven lines. "The eyes…well, they're not as sharp as they used to be."

He shot Tertius a wry glance, the kind of look that almost dared the younger man to laugh. "But that's the point, isn't it? They'll see these words and know it's me, imperfections and all."

Paul's eyes fixed on the parchment for a moment, his fingers grasping the reed pen. Then he turned his gaze to the jar sitting under the window, its restored form bathed in the lamplight. Its scars were unmistakable, a testament to its broken past and painstaking reconstruction. As he looked at it, thoughts crystallized in his mind.

Tertius watched quietly as Paul's eyes returned to the parchment. **"THOSE WHO ARE TRYING TO FORCE YOU TO BE CIRCUMCISED WANT TO LOOK GOOD TO OTHERS. THEY DON'T**

WANT TO BE PERSECUTED FOR TEACHING THAT THE CROSS OF CHRIST ALONE CAN SAVE" (6:12).

Tertius' mind raced as he saw the contrast Paul was making. While the Judaizers wanted to look good to the world, Paul was willing to suffer with Christ for the sake of the cross.

Paul continued, his brow furrowed in concentration. Each word seemed to carry the immensity of his own battle-scarred life: "**AND EVEN THOSE WHO ADVOCATE CIRCUMCISION DON'T KEEP THE WHOLE LAW THEMSELVES. THEY ONLY WANT YOU TO BE CIRCUMCISED SO THEY CAN BOAST ABOUT IT AND CLAIM YOU AS THEIR DISCIPLES**" (6:13).

Tertius reflected on what Paul had shared about his former life—a Pharisee, zealous and rigid, unmatched in his devotion to the law. This wasn't a man swayed by outward displays of righteousness. Paul had seen through the Judaizers from the start. For them, it wasn't about genuine faith or holiness—it was about influence, power, and flaunting their success in persuading others.

The more Tertius thought about it, the more grotesque it seemed—boasting over another man's flesh as if it were a trophy. It was a world apart from the life-transforming power of the gospel Paul preached.

Paul's hand moved across the parchment with deliberate force: "**AS FOR ME, MAY I NEVER BOAST ABOUT ANYTHING EXCEPT THE CROSS OF OUR LORD JESUS CHRIST. BECAUSE OF THAT CROSS, MY INTEREST IN THIS WORLD HAS BEEN CRUCIFIED, AND THE WORLD'S INTEREST IN ME HAS ALSO DIED**" (6:14).

The Judaizers boasted in outward acts, their empty self-righteousness. Yet Paul, more accomplished than any of them, chose to boast only in the suffering and shame of the cross. It was the exact opposite of what the Judaizers sought—a beauty the world rejected.

Dipping the reed pen into the ink again, Paul pressed forward: "**IT DOESN'T MATTER WHETHER WE HAVE BEEN CIRCUMCISED**

or not. What counts is whether we have been transformed into a new creation" (6:15).

Tertius scanned the words. This was the culmination of everything Paul had been saying. The world, with its rules, rituals, and outward markers, suddenly felt empty. The Judaizers were fixated on circumcision and religious acts, but Paul was pointing to something far greater.

The realization hit Tertius like a flood of light. The "new creation" wasn't just about personal change—it was a cosmic shift, the breaking in of a new era. Through the cross, believers were no longer bound to the old world and its values. They belonged to a new creation, defined not by outward signs like circumcision but by the inward reality of being made new in Christ.

Paul continued, **"May God's peace and mercy be upon all who live by this principle; they are the new people of God"** (6:16).

Tertius saw the irony in Paul's words. The Judaizers claimed that peace with God came through strict adherence to the law, yet their path led only to bondage. True peace and mercy came through the cross—through faith—by living as the new creation, transformed by the Spirit.

Paul's point was unmistakable: Being part of God's true family wasn't about outward signs or rules but about walking in the Spirit, just as Jesus did.

Paul's eyes narrowed. He steadied himself as he wrote, his grip tightening against the fatigue creeping into his fingers: **"From now on, don't let anyone trouble me with these things. For I bear on my body the scars that show I belong to Jesus"** (6:17).

As Tertius read the words forming on the parchment, a lump rose in his throat. His eyes lingered on the phrase, unable to look away. He had heard the stories—the beatings, the lashes, the stoning that left Paul for dead. But now, seeing Paul's own unsteady hand etch those words, it became real in a way it never had before.

Paul bore scars, but they weren't just wounds. They were brands.

Slaves were marked by their masters—seared by hot iron, flesh burned to declare ownership.

Roman soldiers carried the insignia of their legion, permanently scarred into their skin.

Criminals, outcasts—society labeled them with marks that could never be erased.

But Paul bore a different kind of mark. He had been whipped, chained, crushed beneath stones, his body broken and remade in suffering. Every scar, every welt, every jagged line on his skin was a declaration of love and devotion. He was owned. Not by Rome. Not by Jew or Gentile. But by Christ.

Paul paused, lifting his eyes from the parchment. The room fell silent. His hand, still poised above the page, trembled slightly as if gathering strength for one final thought.

With a steady breath, he dipped the reed pen into the ink once more, his gaze intense and focused. Then, with slow, deliberate strokes, he inscribed the closing words: **"DEAR BROTHERS AND SISTERS, MAY THE GRACE OF OUR LORD JESUS CHRIST BE WITH YOUR SPIRIT. AMEN"** (6:18).

Tertius swallowed hard, a tear slipping down his cheek. His heart swelled with the significance of the moment. This was the final seal, the benediction that would carry the fullness of Paul's love and concern for the Galatians.

Paul paused, letting out a deep sigh as he set the reed pen aside.

For a moment he remained still, his eyes fixed on the ink drying on the parchment. Then he leaned back in his chair, hands resting on the edge of the table. A sense of profound relief washed over him, as if a heavy weight had been lifted from his shoulders.

It was finished.

For weeks, the letter had grown within him, a burden pressing on his heart and mind. The process of delivering had been both painful and exhausting. Yet now, in this quiet room, as if he had given birth to something precious, Paul felt a profound sense of fulfillment and satisfaction.

His spirit, once taut with urgency, now settled into a peaceful calm. The letter was no longer just words in his heart—it was alive, soon to be sent forth to fulfill its purpose.

Paul stood slowly, his joints creaking. He turned to Tertius, still watching with reverence. Paul placed his hands on the young scribe's shoulders, his grip firm yet gentle.

"Well done," he said, his voice carrying a warmth that went straight to Tertius' heart. "I couldn't have done this without you."

Tertius felt a surge of emotion—pride, gratitude, something deeper he couldn't quite name—as Paul pulled him into a firm embrace. He swallowed hard before murmuring, "Thank you, sir."

Paul stepped back, a tired but satisfied smile on his face.

"What's next?" Tertius asked, his eyes scanning the room.

Paul glanced at the letter, the ink still glistening in the lamplight.

"We'll leave the parchment and the jar out to dry overnight," he instructed. "In the morning, if you wish to see the letter off, meet me at first light. We can send it on its way with the courier together."

CHAPTER 36

THE COURIER

PREDAWN CHILL HUNG in the air as Tertius made his way through the courtyard, the muted rustle of olive branches the only sound in the stillness. His breath misted faintly in the dark. The sky was just beginning to hint at the coming light. The aroma of dew-soaked earth mingled with the lingering scent of last night's hearth fires, now reduced to embers in the crisp air.

He approached the familiar cedar door, a faint light slipping through the cracks around the frame.

Tertius pushed the door open, the heavy creak of wood breaking the silence.

Inside, Paul was already there, the oil lamp casting its golden glow over the parchment spread on the table. He looked up.

"Good morning, brother," he said with a gravelly voice—worn thin by the hours he'd spoken the day before, and not yet fully awake.

Tertius returned a tired smile and moved quietly to the scroll. He ran his fingers along its edge, feeling the smooth yet firm texture of the parchment. With careful precision, he began rolling the scroll from the bottom up, ensuring the tension remained even. This wasn't just a simple task; it required skill. A careless motion, an uneven fold, could leave a crease, marring the words painstakingly written.

As the scroll took its cylindrical shape, Tertius secured it with a small leather tie, looping it around the parchment before knotting it with deft fingers.

He turned to Paul, holding out the rolled scroll. To his surprise, Paul didn't take it immediately. Instead, he reached for the jar sitting on the table, took the scroll from Tertius, and slipped it inside the jar. The scroll slid smoothly into place, protected by the curved, earthen walls. Tertius watched, sensing that this common practice held profound meaning in this moment. Scrolls were often kept in jars for preservation, but this felt different—laden with a deeper symbolism.

As Tertius stared at the jar, the realization struck him like lightning. The jar was more than just clay and resin. It was carrying the gospel message, yes, but it was also telling a story—a story of Paul. A man once broken, now restored, his scars visible, holding within him words of grace and truth.

The jar wasn't only about Paul, though. It was telling another story—the story of Paul's relationship with the Galatians and of the Galatian church itself. Once beautiful, like a vessel fresh from the potter's wheel, it had been shattered by false teaching and division. But now here it stood, held together piece by piece. Its scars were not hidden but displayed as marks of healing.

This was Paul's desire for the Galatians—to be pieced back together, their scars transformed into symbols of grace. Inside that jar lay the letter, holding the key to restoring them. Tertius could almost see it: the cracks in their fellowship, filled with words of truth, mended by God's love.

They wrapped the jar carefully in cloth and placed it inside a worn leather sack, which cradled the jar as if aware of the precious cargo it bore. Together, they stepped out into the crisp morning air. The sound of their footsteps broke the silence as they walked to the front of the house.

A lone figure stood waiting beside a sturdy horse—the courier, his silhouette barely visible in the dim light.

Paul stepped forward, grasping the mysterious man's hand in a firm, familiar grip. "Good to see you, my friend."

Turning to Tertius, Paul's eyes twinkled. "Come here, I want you to meet someone." He placed a steady hand on Tertius' back, nudging him forward. "Tertius, this is Titus."

Tertius studied the man before him, his eyes narrowing in realization. A slow smile spread across his face. "Wait...Titus? The one you mentioned in the letter?" His eyes lit up as he grasped Titus' hand with enthusiasm, shaking it as if greeting an old friend.

Titus chuckled, shaking his head. "Oh my...what has Paul been saying about me?"

Paul waved a dismissive hand. "Oh, it was just a little mention of our trip to Jerusalem."

"Ah, *that* trip," Titus said. He shot Paul a wry glance. "Where I almost lost a part of myself."

Paul snorted in laughter and smacked Titus' shoulder playfully.

Tertius exhaled in understanding as he glanced back at Paul. "A brilliant move—having someone who's an eyewitness to your account deliver the letter in person!"

Paul met Tertius' gaze with a small, satisfied smile. "That's why I didn't say much about it in the letter. Titus, your firsthand account will reinforce what I've written."

Tertius shook his head. "I should have seen this coming. Paul, you've thought of everything."

Paul placed the sack into Titus' hands. The weight of it shifted between them—a silent acknowledgment of the mission ahead.

"Thank you for agreeing to this task," Paul said, his tone quieter now. "This letter carries more than words. It carries the future of the church. Take it with care."

Titus nodded, his expression serious as he slipped the sack into a carrying pouch fastened to the saddle. With a firm grip on the reins, he prepared to mount his horse. Before he could, Paul said, "Let's pray," placing a hand on each man's shoulder. They all bowed their heads.

"Father," Paul began, his voice a mix of urgency and hope. "We ask for Your hand upon this message. May it break through lies, heal divisions, and restore the truth of Your grace."

Tertius nodded, his heart swelling with the richness of Paul's words, silently adding his own prayers.

Titus squeezed his eyes shut, feeling the significance of the task he was about to undertake.

"Let this letter be more than ink on parchment," Paul continued, "but a living word that brings life and freedom to all who read it." He paused, as if the prayer reached out beyond that moment, to the countless lives that would one day be touched by those words.

"We ask these things in the name of Your Son, Jesus our Lord," Paul finished quietly.

"Amen," Tertius and Titus echoed, their voices mingling in the stillness of the early morning.

With that, Titus mounted his horse. He gave a final nod to Paul and Tertius before turning toward the road. As he rode off in the fading darkness, Paul and Tertius stood in silence, watching until his figure disappeared into the mist, leaving behind a mix of heaviness and hope.

Paul turned to Tertius, a rare softness in his eyes. "You know, I really enjoyed this," he said. "I felt God's grace with us as we worked."

Tertius grinned. "Perhaps we'll do it again someday, sir."

A PERSONAL INVITATION

HOW COULD WE come to the end of a book like this without offering you the same invitation Paul gave the Galatians? After all, the heartbeat of Galatians isn't just a history lesson. It's a call—a call to receive the grace of God and be set free.

You see, every one of us, no matter how good or well-intentioned, stands guilty before a holy God. Our best efforts, our moral checklists, our religious to-do lists—they'll never be enough. We've all sinned. We've all fallen short. But Galatians tells us something amazing: God didn't leave us there. He didn't look at our failings and turn away. No, He sent His Son, Jesus Christ, to do what we could never do.

Jesus lived a life without sin. He perfectly fulfilled the law. Then He willingly gave Himself as a sacrifice, taking on our guilt and shame. When He died on the cross, He paid the penalty for our sin in full. And when He rose from the grave, He opened the door to a brand-new life—a life of freedom, a life empowered by His Spirit.

This is what Paul was so passionate about. This is why he wrote with urgency and fire. It's not about what we can achieve. It's not about earning God's favor or trying to be good enough. It's about believing—really trusting—that Jesus did it all. He finished the work. All that's left is for us to receive His gift.

So now, as you turn the last page of this book, the invitation is right here in front of you. Are you ready to lay down your striving? Are you ready to stop trying to earn what can only be received by grace? Are you ready to trust Jesus—not just in theory, but with your whole heart?

If you are, you can pray something like this:

> *God, I know I've fallen short. I am a sinner. I need You. I need Your grace. I believe that Jesus died for me. I believe He rose again. And I believe He's offering me forgiveness and freedom. So I put my trust in Him. I accept His gift. I ask You to come into my life, to fill me with Your Spirit, and to help me live as Your child. Thank You for loving me. In Jesus' name, amen.*

ACKNOWLEDGMENTS

THIS BOOK BEGAN as a sermon series at Nations Church in Orlando, Florida, and I want to thank my church family for being the kind of people who love the Word and hunger for truth. Your faith, encouragement, and passion for Jesus gave me the freedom to preach boldly—and the inspiration to turn those messages into this book. I'm grateful to serve among you.

A heartfelt thank you to Dr. Steve Alt, whose sharp mind and pastoral heart helped guide this manuscript with wisdom and clarity. Steve, your insights helped me stay grounded in the text and faithful to Paul's intent. You've been both an editor and a trusted theological compass.

To my wife, Elizabeth, and children—Elijah, Gloria, London, Lydia, and Benjamin (with one on the way)—thank you for your patience, support, and understanding through the long nights and early mornings of writing. Your love makes every sacrifice worth it.

To my parents—Dan and Liz. Thank you for raising me to love God, to value truth, and to follow Jesus no matter the cost. The seeds you planted long ago continue to bear fruit.

To my spiritual father and mentor, Reinhard Bonnke—thank you for showing me what it means to preach the gospel with fire and to trust God without limits. Your and Anni's legacy lives on in everything I do.

To Peter and Evangeline Vandenberg—your friendship, wisdom, and unwavering support through every season have meant more than words can say. Peter, thank you for standing beside me when the torch was passed and for helping to ensure that the flame would not flicker but burn even brighter.

To the team at Christ for All Nations, thank you for creating a culture that values bold truth and Spirit-empowered ministry. Your example has shaped me in countless ways.

To my best friend and the vice president of our ministry—Russell Benson. Thank you for dreaming with me, building with me, and carrying this vision forward over many years. Your loyalty, insight, and shared fire for the gospel have been an anchor and a gift.

To the amazing team at Charisma Media, thank you for believing in this message and partnering with me to bring it to life. A special thank you to Steve and Joy Strang, for your leadership and vision; to Debbie Marrie, whose guidance and support helped shape this project from the beginning; to Adrienne Gaines, for your wise developmental input; to Ann Mulchan, for navigating the details with clarity and care; to Angie Kiesling, for your editorial insight; and to Makena Song and Claire Kirchner, for your meticulous attention in the final stages. I'm grateful for your excellence, professionalism, and heart for the gospel.

To every friend, mentor, and early reader who offered encouragement or feedback along the way—you know who you are—thank you for believing in the message and helping me bring it to life.

And finally, to the apostle Paul—thank you for fighting for the gospel. Your words still burn with holy fire, and I pray this retelling helps that flame spread a little further.

And now, as Paul might say:

> To the only wise God, through Jesus Christ our Lord—
> be glory, honor, and praise, both now and forever. Amen.

NOTES

Preface

1. Craig S. Keener, *Galatians: A Commentary* (Baker Academic, 2019), xxxiii.
2. Edwald M. Plass, ed., *What Luther Says: A Practical In-Home Anthology for the Active Christian* (Concordia Publishing House, 1959), 989.

Introduction

1. Martyn Lloyd-Jones, *Romans 6: The New Man* (Banner of Truth Trust, 1992).

Chapter 1

1. See Acts 8:1–3; 9:1–2, 13–14.
2. See Acts 9:1–19; 22:3–16; 26:9–18.
3. Paul will directly refer to this in Galatians 1:23.
4. Normally, a first-century letter would be written on papyrus. Parchment was only used for the most important documents. They were more durable but also more expensive. That Paul would use parchment is an indication of how important this letter was.
5. Galatians is the only letter of Paul that lacks a thanksgiving.

Chapter 2

1. The text is taken from the New Living Translation (NLT), except where a change is noted.
2. Paul regularly used the opening greeting to introduce ideas that would be covered in detail later in the letter.
3. Scholars debate whether Paul's letter to the Galatians was addressed to churches in the northern or southern regions of the Roman province. While some argue for a "North Galatian" theory, suggesting Paul wrote to ethnic Galatians in the more remote northern region, this book follows the "South Galatian" view. This perspective is based on the strong historical and textual evidence that Paul's missionary journeys, as recorded in Acts 13–14, primarily took him through the cities of Pisidian

Antioch, Iconium, Lystra, and Derbe—urban centers in the Roman province of Galatia. Since these were the churches Paul established and revisited, it is likely they were the intended recipients of his letter.

4. In this, Paul hints at a major theme of this letter. The gospel rescues people from this present evil world. Paul will later argue that the gospel frees people from the fundamental elements of this world, and by extension, from the law.

CHAPTER 3

1. The Greek word for *gospel* means "good news," but Paul makes it clear that the Judaizers' message is no gospel at all. The wording of the Greek text denies their teaching any place within the apostolic gospel. Though they may have claimed to preach a more Jewish-centered version, like that of Peter and James, Paul rejects this outright. Their message is not good news—it is a distortion that turns freedom into bondage.
2. Paul's *anathema* (Gal. 1:8–9) is not a personal curse but a declaration of divine judgment. In the Old Testament, it signified destruction for defilement (Deut. 7:26; Josh. 6:17–18), paralleling Deuteronomy's blessings and curses. His repetition reinforces certainty, not new condemnation, while including himself and angels underscores that no authority overrides the gospel. This rebuts claims that he still preached circumcision (Gal. 5:11), affirming salvation by faith alone. Galatians 3:10–14 clarifies that the real curse is reliance on the law, which exposed sin but never saved; only Christ *became a curse for us* (Gal. 3:13). Thus, Paul states that false teachers remain condemned, aligning with John 3:18—"Whoever does not believe is condemned already."
3. Gen. 3:8
4. Gen. 3:21
5. John 1:29. John's Gospel had not been written at the time Paul wrote Galatians, but the tradition of John's confession of Jesus was probably well known from the earliest days of the church.
6. John 3:36

CHAPTER 4

1. In the ancient world, broken pottery shards, known as *ostraca*, were commonly used as a writing surface for quick notes,

receipts, and informal records. Unlike papyrus or parchment, which were expensive, ostraca were widely available and durable. While there is no direct evidence that Paul used pottery for writing, it is possible that scribes or early Christians used ostraca for drafting or recording short excerpts before committing them to parchment.

2. An amphora is a tall jar with a narrow neck and two handles.
3. Acts 16:1–3
4. The *God-fearers* were Gentiles who worshipped the God of Israel and respected Jewish teachings but had not fully converted to Judaism. They attended synagogue, observed certain Jewish customs, and lived morally upright lives according to Jewish law. However, they stopped short of full conversion, often because it required circumcision and complete adherence to the Mosaic Law. Many God-fearers were drawn to the message of Jesus because it offered them full inclusion in God's family through faith alone, rather than through circumcision and works of the law.
5. Ezek. 18:4
6. Lev. 17:11
7. This is a point Paul will make in Galatians 2:20.

Chapter 5

1. Tarsus, now a city in modern-day Turkey, was a major trade hub in the Roman province of Cilicia, near the Mediterranean coast.
2. At this time, in his pre-conversion life, Paul was fulfilling Jesus' prophecy in John 16:2: "Those who kill you will think they are doing a holy service for God."
3. Cf. Acts 6:15
4. Cf. Acts 7:55
5. Acts 7:56, NIV
6. Acts 7:60, NIV
7. Luke 23:34
8. The story of Saul's conversion is told in Acts 9:1–19; 22:3–16; 26:9–18.
9. Saul, also called Paul, was known by both names—*Saul* being his Hebrew name and *Paul* his Roman name. The shift occurs in Acts 13:9, during his first missionary journey, when Luke writes, "But Saul, who was also called Paul…" From that point on, Paul is the only name used in Scripture. Unlike Abram becoming

Abraham or Jacob becoming Israel, this was not a divine name change. Instead, Paul likely used his Roman name to better connect with the Gentile world, as his mission expanded beyond the Jewish community.

CHAPTER 6

1. The Nabateans were Arab peoples who lived in what is present-day northwest Saudi Arabia, Jordan, and southern Syria. They spoke Aramaic and Arabic. Paul's preaching to them at this time is likely why he had to narrowly escape their hands by being lowered in a basket (2 Cor. 11:32–33).
2. While Paul states in Galatians 1:17 that he went to Arabia, the Bible does not specify where in Arabia he traveled or what he did there. Some scholars argue that he may have gone to Mount Sinai, following in the footsteps of Moses (Exodus 19–20) and Elijah (1 Kings 19:8–9), both of whom encountered God there. This interpretation gains further weight from Galatians 4:25, where Paul explicitly links Sinai with Arabia. If Paul did travel to Sinai, it would be fitting, as his revelation of the gospel was fundamentally tied to the law. Just as the law was given at Sinai, Paul may have received a deeper revelation of Christ as the fulfillment of the law in the very place where it was first established. This would mirror the pattern of biblical figures encountering God in the wilderness, marking a transition in their calling.
3. See Exod. 19:12–13, 16–19; Heb. 12:18–21.
4. In this narrative, creative license has been taken to place Paul at Sinai. However, this is not the prevailing scholarly view. Craig S. Keener and E. P. Sanders, for example, argue that Paul likely did not travel as far as Sinai. Given that Sinai was roughly four hundred miles from Damascus—a journey that would have required significant resources and at least a month of travel—this scenario appears less probable. Additionally, the fact that Paul later returned to Damascus suggests he likely remained in the Nabatean region, which was much closer and inhabited by the Arabian people. Keener notes that Paul emphasizes solitude in his account, which would align more with retreating into the nearby wilderness rather than embarking on an arduous trek to Sinai.

(Keener, *Galatians*, 260, citing E. P. Sanders, *Paul: The Apostle's Life, Letters, and Thought* [Fortress, 2015], 90.)

5. Phil. 3:7–8
6. Paul refers to his many supernatural experiences with God in 2 Corinthians 12:1–4, 7.

Chapter 7

1. The phrase ἐνώπιον τοῦ Θεοῦ (*enōpion tou Theou*) literally means "in the presence of God" or "before God," invoking God as a direct witness to his truthfulness. In Jewish tradition, swearing an oath before God was an act of utmost seriousness (Num. 30:2; Deut. 23:21–23). False oaths carried divine consequences (Lev. 19:12), and the prophets frequently used similar language to emphasize the weight of their words (Jer. 5:2; Amos 6:8). Even in Roman and Greek legal systems, invoking a deity as a witness to one's truthfulness was a binding declaration, carrying both legal and social consequences if violated.
2. Paul, while cautioning against careless oaths (Matt. 5:34–37), invokes one here to underscore the gravity of his claim—as he does in several other places (Rom. 9:1; 2 Cor. 1:23; Gal. 1:20; Phil. 1:8; 1 Thess. 2:5, 10). The Judaizers accused him of preaching a gospel derived from human sources—particularly the apostles in Jerusalem. By calling God as his witness, Paul makes it unmistakably clear: His message did not come from men but from Christ Himself. This oath is not mere rhetoric; it is a solemn declaration of divine accountability, used as legal testimony to silence false accusations.
3. Matt. 5:34

Chapter 8

1. Paul's timeline of events leading up to the Jerusalem Council is debated. Galatians 1:18 mentions his first visit to Jerusalem "three years" after his conversion, and Galatians 2:1 states he returned "fourteen years later." Some scholars take the "fourteen years" as counting from his conversion (placing this visit around AD 46–47, aligning with the famine relief visit in Acts 11:27–30), while others take it as fourteen years after his first visit (placing it around AD 49–50, aligning with the Jerusalem Council

in Acts 15). The exact timeline remains a subject of scholarly discussion.
2. This story is recounted in Acts 10.
3. This account is given in Acts 11:1–18.
4. Acts 15:1
5. Acts 15:3

CHAPTER 9

1. The dating of Paul's meeting in Galatians 2:1–10 remains a subject of scholarly debate. Some argue it corresponds to the famine relief visit (Acts 11:27–30, ca. AD 46–47), as suggested by F. F. Bruce and Ronald Fung, based on Paul's reference to "fourteen years" (Gal. 2:1) counted from his conversion. However, others, including J. B. Lightfoot, Richard N. Longenecker, and Craig S. Keener, contend that it aligns with the Jerusalem Council (Acts 15:1–29, ca. AD 49–50), given the thematic parallels concerning circumcision and Gentile inclusion. A third position, advocated by Philip Esler and James D. G. Dunn, proposes a private meeting preceding the council, explaining Paul's emphasis on a confidential discussion (Gal. 2:2) while still fitting within the broader Acts 15 context. This interpretation is the basis for our narrative.
2. The identity of these "false brothers" (ψευδαδέλφους, *pseudadelphous*) in Galatians 2:4 is debated. Some believe they were Pharisaic believers mentioned in Acts 15:5—Christians who sincerely, though wrongly, believed Gentiles had to follow the Law of Moses. Others argue they were Judaizers who didn't truly follow Christ but infiltrated the church to push legalism. Paul seems to see them as deceivers, not just mistaken believers—which is why he refers to them so strongly.
3. Titus' presence at this meeting is significant because he was an uncircumcised Gentile Christian. The Judaizers likely saw him as a test case—if he was pressured into circumcision, it would set a precedent that all Gentiles must follow the law to be accepted in the church. However, Acts 15 does not mention Titus by name, which has led some scholars to suggest that this incident in Galatians 2:3–5 happened before or during the broader council discussion.
4. Cf. 1 Cor. 12:12–26

Chapter 12

1. Belief in a personal God who cared about the individual worshipper was rare. More common was to view God as someone to bargain with or make a deal with, whether through sacrifice or supplication. Paul's description of his relationship with God is rare in the ancient world, even in Judaism.

Chapter 13

1. In Galatians 3:1, Paul says Christ was "clearly portrayed as crucified" before their eyes. The Greek *proegraphē* (προεγράφη) suggests a vivid public display. Paul's preaching was so clear it was as if they had seen Christ crucified themselves, making their drift into legalism all the more baffling.
2. Quoting Genesis 15:6.
3. He was seventy-five years old when he came to Canaan (Gen. 12:40), and at least a few years passed before God issued this promise in Genesis 15.
4. Quoting Genesis 12:3.

Chapter 14

1. The Book of Galatians was likely written around AD 48–50, whereas Acts, authored by Luke, was composed much later, likely between AD 62–70. This means that while the story of Pentecost was widely known through oral tradition, it had not yet been formally documented. Paul's fictional remark in this scene reflects the reality that key moments in early church history were still being passed down by word of mouth rather than preserved in written accounts.

Chapter 15

1. Num. 11:24–30
2. Num. 11:29
3. Deuteronomy 18:15. Peter quotes this verse in a sermon in Acts 3:22, identifying Jesus as the fulfillment.
4. 2 Kings 2:9–12
5. Ezek. 36:26–27
6. Isa. 44:3
7. Joel 2:28–32

8. Matt. 3:11; Luke 3:16. Cf. Mark 1:8, which does not mention fire.
9. John 14:16–17, 26; 15:26; 16:7. The NLT refers to him as the Advocate.
10. Matthew 27; Mark 15; Luke 23; John 19. Darkness is mentioned in Matthew 27:45; Mark 15:33; Luke 23:44–45. An earthquake is mentioned in Matthew 27:51.
11. Luke 24:49
12. The phrase "the whole house" (Acts 2:2) likely refers to the temple, not a private upper room, as the temple was commonly called "the house of the Lord" (1 Kings 8:10–11; Mal. 3:1). Luke uses this language in Luke 19:46 when Jesus calls the temple "a house of prayer" (quoting Isaiah 56:7). Several clues support this view: The large crowd in Acts 2:6 gathered too quickly for a private home setting; Pentecost was a major pilgrimage feast where worshippers would have already been assembled at the temple (Deut. 16:16), and the baptism of three thousand people (Acts 2:41) would have been far more feasible at the temple's mikvehs (ritual immersion pools); the imagery of wind and fire (Acts 2:2–3) also parallels past theophanies at the tabernacle and temple (Exod. 19:16–18; 2 Chron. 7:1–3). A likely scenario is that the disciples began in the upper room but moved to the temple for morning prayers, where the Spirit was poured out, drawing the crowd and setting the stage for Peter's sermon.
13. Acts 2:41

Chapter 16

1. If it were not permanent, Jesus would not have been able to say, "I am with you always, even to the end of the age" (Matt. 28:20).
2. As Jesus told the disciples: "He lives with you now and later will be in you" (John 14:17; cf. 1 Cor. 6:19).
3. Acts 17:28

Chapter 17

1. Paul's quotation is from Genesis 12:3, as also quoted in Galatians 3:8.
2. Deut. 27:26. Paul quotes from the Greek translation, the Septuagint (LXX). He makes a few minor alterations, none of which alter the meaning of the verse. For a look at the changes, see Richard N. Longenecker, *Galatians, Word Biblical*

Commentary vol. 41, David A. Hubbard and Glenn W. Barker, eds. (Word, 1990), 117.

3. *Devarim*, meaning "Words," is the Hebrew name for the Book of Deuteronomy. It was used in Paul's day, as the book was traditionally referred to by its Hebrew title. The term *Deuteronomy* (meaning "second law") came later through the Greek translation. I use *Devarim* in this narrative to reflect the terminology familiar to Paul and his contemporaries.
4. Ezek. 18:9
5. This reference is based on a story about Rabban Gamaliel II (the great-grandson of Gamaliel I), who is said to have wept over the verse due to the impossibility of perfectly keeping the law. However, Rabbi Akiba interpreted Leviticus 18:24 to suggest that avoiding the most serious sins, such as adultery and idolatry, was sufficient to maintain righteousness under the law. While we cannot definitively trace this interpretation back to Gamaliel I (the Elder), it is known that in the first century some believed it was possible to live in such a way as to be considered righteous according to the law. Notably, when Paul quotes Deuteronomy 27:26, he contrasts it with a passage from Leviticus 18, highlighting the different approaches to righteousness.
6. *Ostraca* (singular: *ostracon*) were broken pottery shards repurposed as writing surfaces in the ancient world. Due to the expense of papyrus and parchment, these fragments were commonly used for informal notes, receipts, letters, and even legal records. Scribes and scholars often etched or inked text onto ostraca for temporary writings or personal study. Archaeological discoveries have uncovered ostraca with everything from tax records to biblical texts, demonstrating their widespread use in daily life.
7. Paul is contrasting Habakkuk 2:4 with Leviticus 18:5.
8. Quoting Deuteronomy 21:23.

Chapter 18

1. While the NLT translates the term as "descendants" in Genesis and "child" in Galatians, the word *offspring* is preferred here because it more accurately reflects the singular and collective nature of the original Hebrew and Greek terms. Paul's explanation hinges on the singular form, emphasizing that the

promise to Abraham points to one specific descendant—Jesus Christ—through whom all nations would be blessed. The term *offspring* better preserves this nuance, whereas *child* in Galatians obscures this distinction.

2. The noun is a collective singular, so it could be interpreted as plural. Judaism generally did this, believing the promises were fulfilled in all the descendants of Abraham. But there is a tradition in Judaism that interpreted the promise to be fulfilled in Isaac, which supports Paul's interpretation that a singular descendant fulfills the promise.
3. John 1:32–34
4. Cf. 2 Cor. 1:22; Eph. 1:13–14
5. The original word here is *offspring* (Hebrew *zera*, Greek *sperma*), which is grammatically singular but understood as a collective term referring to many people. Historically, Jews interpreted it as referring to multiple descendants, which is why Paul had to clarify that it refers to a singular descendant in this passage. This is also why we prefer *offspring* or *seed* over *child*, as most translations use these terms to reflect the singular/plural nuance. In fact, the NLT translates the noun in the plural form in Genesis 12:7; 13:15; 17:8; and 24:7, the passages Paul alludes to here.

CHAPTER 19

1. The Pentateuch never names Moses as a mediator, but it does say it was given "in the hand of Moses" (Exod. 34:29; Lev. 26:46; Num. 4:37–49). First-century Judaism taught that Moses mediated the covenant (1 Esdras 9:39; Testament of Moses 1:14; Philo, Life of Moses, 2.166). No doubt, Tertius was schooled in this tradition.
2. Gen. 15:7–21
3. Paul's interpretation of the Abrahamic covenant as unilateral aligns with Jewish thought of the time. Texts such as Jubilees 15:4–9, Psalms of Solomon 9:8–11, and Wisdom of Solomon 10:5, along with writings from Philo and the Dead Sea Scrolls (Genesis Apocryphon and Community Rule), emphasize God's sovereign initiative and grace in establishing the covenant. These sources present the covenant as eternal, implying its unbreakable nature, which inherently suggests it is unconditional.

Chapter 20

1. Craig Keener's summary of Norman Young's extensive study on the pedagogue interprets Paul's use of the pedagogue analogy as twofold: "It was temporary and it included restrictive guarding of the boy" (Keener, *Galatians*, 573).
2. The first-century Jewish work Letter of Aristeas confirms Judaism's view of the law as a "fence" that surrounds the people of God, protecting them from the dangers of the pagan world around them.
3. Some interpreters see Paul's reference to "protective custody" as entirely positive, and Paul would agree with the positive aspects of it. But as the surrounding context makes clear, it also has a negative side, which is why Paul can use the language of slavery to refer to it in the verses that follow (4:1–5).
4. In proving that Gentiles are children of God, Paul proves that they are full inheritors, implying that circumcision will gain nothing for them. It also implies that Jewish believers can have full fellowship with Gentile believers, since they are siblings. That further implies that all foods are clean. If they weren't, Jewish and Gentile believers could not eat together.
5. The Greek word *stoicheion* (στοιχεῖον), translated here as "basic spiritual principles," is a debated term. It can mean "elementary principles" (basic teachings or fundamental structures of thought), "elemental forces" (the natural elements), or even refer to spiritual beings in certain contexts. Some scholars believe Paul is referring to human religious systems (both Jewish and pagan) that kept people in bondage, while others argue he is referring to demonic influences that enslave the world. The Greek text does not explicitly include the word *spiritual*, so some translations prefer "elementary principles" or "elemental forces" instead.

Chapter 21

1. Paul's phrase "weak and miserable forces" (Greek: *stoicheia tou kosmou*) refers to both spiritual powers and human religious systems that enslave. The term *stoicheia* can mean elemental principles, natural forces, or even spiritual beings, depending on the context. Some translations (like the NLT) use "spiritual principles," but this may be misleading, as the Greek word does not inherently imply anything spiritual. Paul likely had

in mind both the legalistic systems of Judaism and the pagan hierarchies of the Gentile world—both of which enslaved people through systems of performance, law, and ritual. His point is clear: Any structure, whether religious or spiritual, that requires human effort for righteousness is a return to bondage. See Galatians 4:3, 9; Colossians 2:8, 20; and compare with Ephesians 6:12. (Douglas J. Moo, *Galatians* [BECNT, 2013], 275–278; N. T. Wright, *Paul and the Faithfulness of God* [Fortress, 2013], 845–848; Keener, *Galatians*, 319–321.)

2. It is possible that when Paul says the Galatians treated him "as an angel of God" (Gal. 4:14), he is referencing not only their kindness but also a well-known local legend. According to Metamorphoses by Ovid (Book 8), Zeus and Hermes once visited a Phrygian town disguised as beggars, seeking hospitality. The townspeople repeatedly rejected them, except for an elderly couple, Philemon and Baucis, who welcomed them. As a result, the gods destroyed the city, sparing only the couple. This story was widely known in the region and may explain why the people of Lystra, upon witnessing Paul's miracles despite his physical weakness, initially treated him and Barnabas as divine messengers (Acts 14:8–18). Their hospitality, at least in part, may have been driven by the fear of making the same mistake as their ancestors.

CHAPTER 22

1. The source of Paul's illness in Galatians 4:13 is debated, with some suggesting a chronic condition and others a temporary ailment. This narrative explores the possibility that Paul was still recovering from his stoning in Lystra (Acts 14:19–20). Although Lystra was within Galatia, the text does not specify where he first preached in weakness. Since he continued traveling, it's reasonable to assume his recovery extended into cities like Iconium or Pisidian Antioch. This interpretation aligns with Galatians 4:15, where the Galatians' willingness to give Paul their own eyes may hint at lingering vision issues from his injuries. This framing remains historically plausible while adding dramatic depth to his emotional appeal.
2. The phrase "you did not scorn or despise me" in Galatians 4:14 contains the Greek verb ἐξεπτύσατε (*exeptysate*), which means

"to spit out" or "reject." In the ancient world, spitting was a common way to ward off the "evil eye," a superstition used to protect against curses or bad luck. If the Galatians had believed Paul was cursed or under an evil influence, they might have instinctively spat when they saw him—but they didn't. This suggests they fully accepted him at first. Later, in Galatians 3:1, Paul asks, "Who has bewitched you?" possibly linking their change in attitude to the same superstition. Even if their hesitation was due to Paul's physical wounds rather than fear of a curse, his suffering still tested their willingness to receive him (Keener, *Galatians*, 378–379).

3. In Galatians 3:1, Paul's phrase "Who has bewitched you?" (NKJV) comes from the Greek τίς ὑμᾶς ἐβάσκανεν (*tis hymas ebaskanen*). The verb βασκαίνω (*baskaino*) is closely tied to the ancient belief in the evil eye (see previous endnote). While most translations render it as "bewitched" to emphasize deception, the original wording may carry the idea of someone casting the evil eye upon the Galatians—a pointed irony, considering that Paul himself had been accused of carrying a curse due to his afflicted eyes (Gal. 4:13–15). This theme of the evil eye as both a superstition and a spiritual metaphor will reappear later in Paul's argument.

Chapter 23

1. Abraham's age is given in Genesis 16:16.
2. Gen. 16:4–6
3. Gen. 16:9–10
4. Abraham was ninety-nine when God said Isaac would be born "about this time next year" (Gen. 17:21), making him one hundred years old when Isaac was born.
5. Gen. 21:9–10
6. The quotation is from Isaiah 54:1.
7. Translations often render the verb in Genesis 21:9 as "mocking," or something similar. But linguists claim the word probably just means "laughing" or "playing." Judaism interpreted it negatively, though, and Paul is referring to their interpretation here, probably because this is how the Judaizers interpreted it. This would be called an ad hominem argument, where Paul argues based on what his opponents believe, even if it is erroneous.
8. Quoting Genesis 21:10.

CHAPTER 24

1. Raised as a faithful Jew, Paul would have been taught to regard the law as a blessing and living under it as a joy. But here his perspective reflects the inability of anyone to perfectly keep it, resulting in falling under its curse. The demands crush because no one can keep them.

CHAPTER 25

1. See Romans 7:6, using the same word, *katargeo*, that he uses in Galatians 5:4.
2. This is a point made by Keener, *Galatians*, 732, following Moo, *Galatians*, 326.
3. See Ezek. 18:24, 26; 33:12–13, 18.

CHAPTER 26

1. Paul uses the analogy of running a race in 1 Corinthians 9:24–27 and Philippians 3:12–14. He uses the analogy of yeast leavening the whole batch of dough in 1 Corinthians 5:6.
2. Mark 8:15–21
3. This is a synonym for yeast.
4. Some accused Paul of preaching circumcision, likely due to his decision to circumcise Timothy (Acts 16:3). However, Paul clarifies that if he still upheld circumcision for salvation, the Judaizers wouldn't oppose him. His persecution proves he preaches justification by faith alone, not the law (Gal. 5:2–4).
5. Deuteronomy 23:1 forbids any man who has been castrated from entering the assembly of the Lord. The Greek translation of this verse, the Septuagint, uses the same word that Paul uses for "mutilate" (*apokoptō*), and the word for "assembly" is *ekklēsia*, the same word the NT uses for "church."

CHAPTER 27

1. The Greek word *sarx* in Galatians 5:13 is best translated as "flesh," yet the NLT renders it "sinful nature," a lexically inaccurate and theologically misleading choice. Nearly all major translations—including the ESV, NASB, CSB, and the NIV after its 2011 revision—have corrected this mistake. Paul's use of *sarx* is intentional, carrying both a literal and spiritual

meaning: Circumcision is a matter of the flesh, yet trusting in it for righteousness places one under its power. By replacing "sinful nature" with "flesh" here and in 5:16, 17, 19, 24, and 6:8, 12, this translation preserves Paul's wordplay and theological depth—contrasting the works of the flesh with the freedom of the Spirit. To miss this is to weaken both Paul's argument and the rhetorical force of his words.

2. Loving your neighbor as yourself is taught in Leviticus 19:18. It was an important part of Jesus' teaching too (Matt. 22:39; Mark 12:31; Luke 10:27). Paul also taught it in Romans 13:9.
3. Rom. 7:14
4. Rom. 8:8
5. See Keener, *Galatians*, 1,027. Hillel, the Elder (d. 10 BC), gave the converse of the golden rule as his epitome of the law: "What is hateful to you, do not do to your fellow. This is the entire Torah; the rest is commentary" (bSabb 31a).

Chapter 28

1. Rom. 8:2
2. Rom. 6:6

Chapter 29

1. This summarizes Paul's teaching in Romans 6:1–14.
2. Cf. Rom. 6:2, 11
3. 1 Corinthians 2:16. Contrary to popular opinion, Paul declares that all believers have the mind of Christ. We just don't all walk in it. The Corinthians, for example, chose to walk in a worldly way instead of living by the Spirit (1 Cor 3:1–2). For more on this, see Gordon D. Fee, *The First Epistle to the Corinthians, NICNT* (Eerdmans, 1987), 119–20.

Chapter 30

1. This is reminiscent of the parable of the Good Samaritan. Three religious leaders passed the man who had been robbed, probably thinking they would be rendered unclean, or just thinking they were too important to be bothered. That the one who helped was a Samaritan suggests the latter. Jews thought they were superior to Samaritans, and Jesus is teaching that they should help anyone in need. This is a practical example of loving one's neighbor.

Chapter 31

1. Rom. 8:20–21

Chapter 32

1. Paul taught that elders who preach and teach should be paid double (1 Tim. 5:17), and he taught that all workers in the gospel should be paid (1 Cor. 9:9)
2. It reminds one of Paul's words to the Corinthians: "We have this treasure in jars of clay" (2 Cor. 4:7).

Chapter 33

1. Perhaps Paul had Hosea 10:12 in mind when he wrote this: "Sow for yourselves righteousness, gather the fruit of life" (LXX). Proverbs 8:11 promises a reward to the one who sows righteousness. This principle is sometimes used with reference to giving financially. Jesus taught that whatever one measures out to others will be measured to them (Luke 6:38), and Paul elsewhere taught that one will receive according to what they give (2 Cor. 9:6).

ABOUT THE AUTHOR

DANIEL KOLENDA IS a missionary evangelist, pastor, author, and teacher who has preached the gospel face-to-face to millions through massive open-air evangelistic campaigns in some of the most dangerous, remote, and spiritually resistant places on earth.

As the successor to world-renowned evangelist Reinhard Bonnke, Kolenda serves as the president and CEO of Christ for all Nations (CfaN)—a global evangelistic ministry that has pioneered some of the largest soul-winning efforts in history. Under his leadership, CfaN has expanded its reach across six continents and has now recorded over 100 million documented decisions for Christ. The ministry has also printed more than 190 million copies of its books in 104 languages and maintains 14 offices in 12 countries.

Kolenda is also the founder and lead pastor of Nations Church in Orlando, Florida—a vibrant, Spirit-filled community launched as a local expression of the global harvest. Through Nations Church, he continues to equip believers, raise up leaders, and shepherd a growing body of Christ-followers with the same urgency and passion that fuel his evangelistic ministry.

Kolenda's passion for multiplying laborers has fueled the Decade of Double Harvest—a bold initiative to raise up thousands of evangelists. Through Gospel Campaigns, the Evangelism Bootcamp, Fire Camps, the CfaN School of Ministry, One2One

Evangelism Training, and Schools of Evangelism around the world, CfaN continues to equip and launch thousands of soul-winners into the field.

He has hosted two internationally broadcast television programs and is the author of several books, including the bestsellers *Live Before You Die* and *Slaying Dragons*. His writing blends theological depth with practical insight and a deep passion for the gospel.

Kolenda lives in Orlando with his wife, Elizabeth, and five children—Elijah, Gloria, London, Lydia, and Benjamin (with one on the way).